SOMETIMES HUNTING CAN SEEM LIKE BUSINESS:

POLAR BEAR SPORT HUNTING IN NUNAVUT

George W. Wenzel

Canadian Circumpolar Institute (CCI) Press
University of Alberta

2008

Library and Archives Canada Cataloguing in Publication

Keywords: Inuit; Polar Bear Sport Hunting; Nunavut; Traditional Knowledge; Socio-Economic Relations; Climate Change

© 2008 CCI Press, University of Alberta

All rights reserved.
No part of this publication may be reproduced, stored in a retrieval system, or transmitted in any form or by any means—electronic, mechanical, photocopying, recording, or otherwise without the express permission of the copyright owner/s. CCI Press is a registered publisher with access© the Canadian Copyright Licensing Agency (Publisher Number 3524)

Cover:
Cover design by art design printing, inc.
Front Cover adapted from image courtesy Martha Dowsley
Back cover photo courtesy CCI Press
Printed in Canada (Edmonton) by art design printing, inc.

This publication was made possible with grant funding from

The author can be reached at (c/o Department of Geography, McGill University, Montreal, Quebec, Canada H3A 2K6

ISBN 978-1-896445-43-4   **ISSN** 0068-0303

Table of Contents

Preface iii
Acknowledgements v

Chapter One:
THE STUDY COMMUNITIES 1
Introduction 1
Community Baseline Information 4
    Clyde River 4
    Resolute 5
    Taloyoak 6
Summary 8

Chapter Two:
POLAR BEARS AS A RESOURCE: AN OVERVIEW 9
Inuit Subsistence 9
The Commodization of Polar Bears: Circa 1850-1970 9
The Business of Polar Bear Sport Hunting: 1970-1985 11
The Contemporary Sport-Hunt: 1985-2000 14
Summary 19

Chapter Three:
INUIT TEK AND THE SPORT HUNT 21
Traditional Ecological Knowledge (TEK) 21
TEK in the Present Research 21
The Management System 22
TEK and Polar Bear Conservation 23
TEK and the Sport-Hunt 24
The TEK Data 26
Traditional Knowledge Summary 31

Chapter Four:
COMMUNITY ORGANIZATION OF THE HUNT 33
An Introductory Perspective 33
Community Dynamics and *Inuit Qaujimajatuqangit* 34
    Resolute Bay 35
    Clyde River 44
    Taloyoak 53

Chapter Five:
SPORT HUNTING AND INUIT SUBSISTENCE 61
Introduction 61
Overview of the Data 61
Pattern of the Analysis 62
The Sport-Hunt's Values and Flows 63

The Southern Data ... 64
The Northern Data ... 67
Section Summary and Observations ... 73

Chapter Six:
COMMUNITY ISSUES ... **77**
Introduction ... 77
Taloyoak and Regulatory Conflict ... 78
Socio-Economic Relations in Resolute Bay ... 79
Clyde River: Hunting Inuktitut ... 80

Chapter Seven:
SPORT HUNT BENEFITS AND COSTS ... **83**
Benefits ... 83
Costs ... 88

Chapter Eight:
MOUs, IQ AND CLIMATE CHANGE ... **91**
Introduction ... 91
Nunavut's Memoranda of Understanding ... 91
Inuit and Biologists ... 92
Climate Change, *IQ* and Sport Hunting vs Polar Bear ... 94
Outcomes ... 95

CONCLUSIONS ... **97**

REFERENCES CITED ... **101**

APPENDICES ... **107**
Appendix One: Recommendations
　　Recommendation to the Government of Nunavut ... 109
　　Additional Recommendations ... 109
Appendix Two:
　　Research Objectives, Data Types, and Methods ... 111
　　The Data ... 111
Appendix Three:
　　Data Collection ... 113

EXTENDED TABLE OF CONTENTS ... **115**
　　List of Tables ... 118
　　List of Figures ... 118
　　Glossary of Frequently Used Abbreviations ... 119

Preface

About the Project

Since the 1980s, when ringed seal skin and other Inuit harvest products lost external market value, polar bear (*Ursus maritimus*) sport hunting has become a significant element in the mixed economies of small Nunavut communities. While highly seasonal, of brief duration, and dependent on a restricted non-Inuit clientele, the sport hunt provides a means for highly skilled Inuit hunters to obtain monies needed to engage in a wide range of subsistence activities important to the food economies of these communities.

This study examines Inuit participation in the hunt, and effects of the sport hunt industry, in the communities of Taloyoak, Resolute and Clyde River. Its foci include the role of Traditional Ecological Knowledge in the hunt, community level organizational dynamics of sport hunting, socio-economic benefits and costs of the hunt, and important social, economic and cultural issues arising from the polar bear sport-hunt. Finally, the new and still emerging dynamic between Inuit and *Qallunaat* regarding polar bear in the light of global climate concerns is reviewed.

This study had its genesis in research undertaken with support from the Government of Nunavut's Department of Sustainable Development and the Safari Club International Foundation (SCIF). This support was in the form of a grant from the Foundation and a Contribution Agreement with the Territorial Government. In addition, supplementary fieldwork in 2006 and 2007 was made possible by support from the Social Sciences and Humanities Research Council of Canada's Northern Research Development Program and ArcticNet and the encouragement of my Co-Principal Investigator, Milton Freeman of the University of Alberta.

The results of that formative work were submitted to the Nunavut Government and the SCIF in a report titled *Outfitted Polar Bear Hunting, Community Economy and Species Conservation in the Kitikmeot and Qikiqtaaluk Regions of Nunavut* (Wenzel and Bourgouin 2003). At the same time, the report in full was made available in Inuktitut and English to the Hunters' and Trappers' Organizations of Resolute Bay, Taloyoak and Clyde River and the Kitikmeot Wildlife Organization (now the Kitikmeot Wildlife Board).

The primary objective of the research was to provide data to both original supporting partners regarding how outfitted, or guided, trophy hunting might be better employed for the management and conservation of the polar bear. Overall, the central intent of the project was to develop baseline information on the economics and organization of the sport-hunt to facilitate the integration of what is often referred to as conservation hunting (Freeman *et al.* 2005; Freeman and Wenzel 2006) into Nunavut's evolving polar bear management regime. It was with this goal that research was undertaken in the communities of Resolute, Clyde and Taloyoak, as well as with non-Inuit sport hunters and hunt wholesalers with experience in Nunavut.

Almost from the time fieldwork began, it also became apparent that, unlike many other types of tourism activities in the North (*see* Milne *et al.* 1997), trophy polar bear hunting brings very large infusions of money into the economies of hosting communities with only minor outflow into southern hands—and does so in a relatively short period of time. Moreover, it was clear that a significant portion of this inflow of money went directly into the hands of Inuit working on sport-hunts as guides and hunt-helpers. As a result of these preliminary observations, data on the socioeconomic and social organizational dynamics of polar bear sport hunting within hosting communities was gathered in order to determine whether such hunting might become a more productive component in local economic development.

That this might be an important, if secondary, objective was hinted at even before the project began, when preliminary research in the files of the Department of Sustainable Development (Bourgouin 1998) revealed that almost no information related to the sport-hunt other than to whom a license was issued (including individuals' home proveniences), and the biological samples related to a successfully hunted animal's sex and age was collected. How much money visitor-hunters paid for their hunts, what part of this fee entered hosting communities, what the wage rates for Inuit involved in the hunt were, and to what purposes sport-hunt income was used by Inuit hunt workers, or any other effects this money may have had within communities, were unknown.

It should also be clear that the research was not conducted with the objective of making recommendations about either the primary or secondary objectives. In that sense, there was no explicit applied aspect intended. On the other hand, following the completion of the research and after submission of its final report, a variety of possible applications of the study's results were discussed with members of the Government of Nunavut and with Inuit in the communities that assisted the project. For completeness sake, these recommendations are presented in Appendix 1. In any case, events beginning in January 2005 made any recommendations flowing from the research moot when the Government of Nunavut's decision to increase the Total Allowable Harvest (TAH) of Polar Bear provoked broad scientific and environmental criticism.

The basic results, on the other hand, remain valid. These were communicated to the Nunavut land claim beneficiaries organization, Nunavut Tunngavik Incorporated, and have since been disseminated through several scholarly articles (Wenzel 2005; Freeman and Wenzel 2006) and academic proceedings (Wenzel and Dowsley 2005; Wenzel et al. 2005).

The overall approach taken to the data that are presented is distinctly qualitative. In no small sense, the analysis presented is much more from an anthropological perspective than it is from that of either conservation biology or economics. Where necessary, information related to characteristics of the Inuit and sport hunters who participated in the study and to elements of polar bear trophy hunting, such as its fee structure and similar features, are presented in a variety of tables and also discussed within the narrative.

These data have not been subjected to formal statistical testing. This is because, in an overall sense, the data are drawn from three very limited, and more than a little fluid, community situations. Because the body of data is heavily time constrained, it should not be read beyond the cases themselves. Notwithstanding these limitations and caveats, the results reflect a fair picture of polar bear trophy hunting in the northern Qikiqtaaluk and eastern Kitikmeot regions of Nunavut until 2005, when new Memoranda of Understanding between the Government of Nunavut and the communities across the territory were signed.

Acknowledgements

This research would have not been possible without the willing assistance of the Hunters' and Trappers' Organizations (HTOs) of Resolute Bay, Taloyoak and Clyde River. Indeed, for the fieldwork at Clyde River to go forward required a vote at the HTOs' Annual General Meeting; thus thanks to those 150 or so affirming members for their support. I also wish to thank the various officers of the Wildlife Division, Department of Sustainable Development—DSD (now Department of Environment), Government of Nunavut, for providing me with access to department databases and to the council of the Safari Club International (SCI) Foundation for its assistance in introducing me to various SCI members and for permitting me to conduct interviews at its 2002 Annual Meeting. The generosity of the Foundation, the Government of Nunavut and the SSHRC in funding this work has already been mentioned. I also thank the members of the Hunters' and Trappers' Organizations of Taloyoak, Resolute and Clyde River, the sport hunters who acceded to my interviews and surveys, the southern wholesalers, and the Inuit outfitters who gave their time to the research when they undoubtedly had much more interesting things to do.

Beyond these organizations, there are many people who deserve individual thanks because of their special efforts. To begin, I sincerely thank Dr. J.Y. Jones of Safari Club International Foundation, Dr. Mitchell Taylor, Department of Sustainable Development, and Dr. Stuart Marks who brought me into contact with J.Y. and Mitch. Without them, there would not have been a project. I also thank Ms. France Bourgouin, who conducted important pre-project archival research in DSD's files and who assisted with the research in Resolute Bay. Ms. Bourgouin also collated the economic data from the communities and drafted thoughts on the economics of the hunt.

None of the community work would have been possible without the help of the many Inuit who provided extensive responses to the research questions, aided in the collection of data, translated for some of the interviews and provided valued companionship. To name just a few, my thanks to Ms. Aliciik Illaut, Mr. Luti Pulluq, Ms. Susan Salluviniq and Mr. Allie Salluviniq of Resolute Bay, Mr. David Irngaut of Taloyoak, Mr. Levi Palituq, Mr. Jamesee Qillaq and Mr. Sam Palituq of Clyde River and Mr. Jonathan Palluq, formerly of Clyde River and now living in Pond Inlet. My thanks also to Ms. Janet Troje and Ms. Laurie-Anne White, both of Iqaluit, for their always-gracious hospitality when suddenly dropped in upon and to Susan Salluviniq for translating the final project report into two dialects of Inuktitut.

Finally, I received encouragement and more than a few helpful criticisms from colleagues at McGill and more far-flung places. To Laurie-Anne White, Mitch Taylor, Wayne Pollard, Martha Dowsley, David Lee and especially Jim Savelle, all of whom waded through early drafts of this work. I hope the final product is not a disappointment.

Chapter One

THE STUDY COMMUNITIES

Introduction

The research focused on three communities that currently host polar bear sport-hunting, or have done so in the recent past. These were Clyde River and Resolute Bay, both in the Qikiqtaaluk (Baffin) Region, and Taloyoak in the Kitikmeot (Central Arctic Coast) Region (Fig. 1).

    Clyde River, Resolute Bay and Taloyoak were chosen for the project for several reasons, while a fourth, Grise Fiord, declined to participate. The central reason for choosing these communities was that the volume of sport-hunt visitors was large enough to have noticeable economic impact. Clyde River and Taloyoak each have a relatively substantial number of residents dependent on social transfers in their respective regions. Resolute Bay, in contrast, has the second lowest rate of participation in the social transfer economy in the Qikiqtaaluk region. However, in light of its small population (the second smallest in the region), the polar bear sport-hunt employs a greater percentage of adults than in either Clyde River or Taloyoak.

    A second reason for selecting these communities was that each utilizes a different, although not absolutely discrete, polar bear population area (Fig. 2). Lack of 'territorial' overlap in hunting areas was seen as a factor likely to reduce response bias due to perceived competition with another study community. Indeed, the chair of the Grise Fiord Hunters' and Trappers' Organization explicitly stated that he saw his community as competing with other sport-hunt sites, and especially with Resolute Bay (J. Akeeagok, pers. comm. 2001).

    A third reason was that a preliminary investigation in the summer of 2000 suggested significant structural differences existed in how the sport-hunt was organized at each locale. This lack of a single, overarching mode of organization provided an opportunity to compare how differences in the allocation of each community's annual quota to the sport-hunt and in hunt worker recruitment might affect social and economic community dynamics.

    The final factor was that the relevant institutional (Nunavut Research Institute, Regional Hunters' and Trappers' Organization) and community (Hamlet Council, local Hunters' and Trappers' Organization) permission required for independent research could be negotiated prior to beginning intensive fieldwork in 2001. This entailed visits to three of the communities (Resolute Bay, Clyde River, and Grise Fiord), while Taloyoak, because of its unique situation regarding the closure of its polar bear sport-hunt, requested inclusion in the research. During these preliminary visits, efforts were made to informally meet with various community members who participated in the local sport-hunt, such as noted guides and local outfitters, in order to discuss the nature of the intended research. However, actual data collection only started in 2001 after the required Nunavut Research License, community permissions, and individual informed consent were actually obtained.

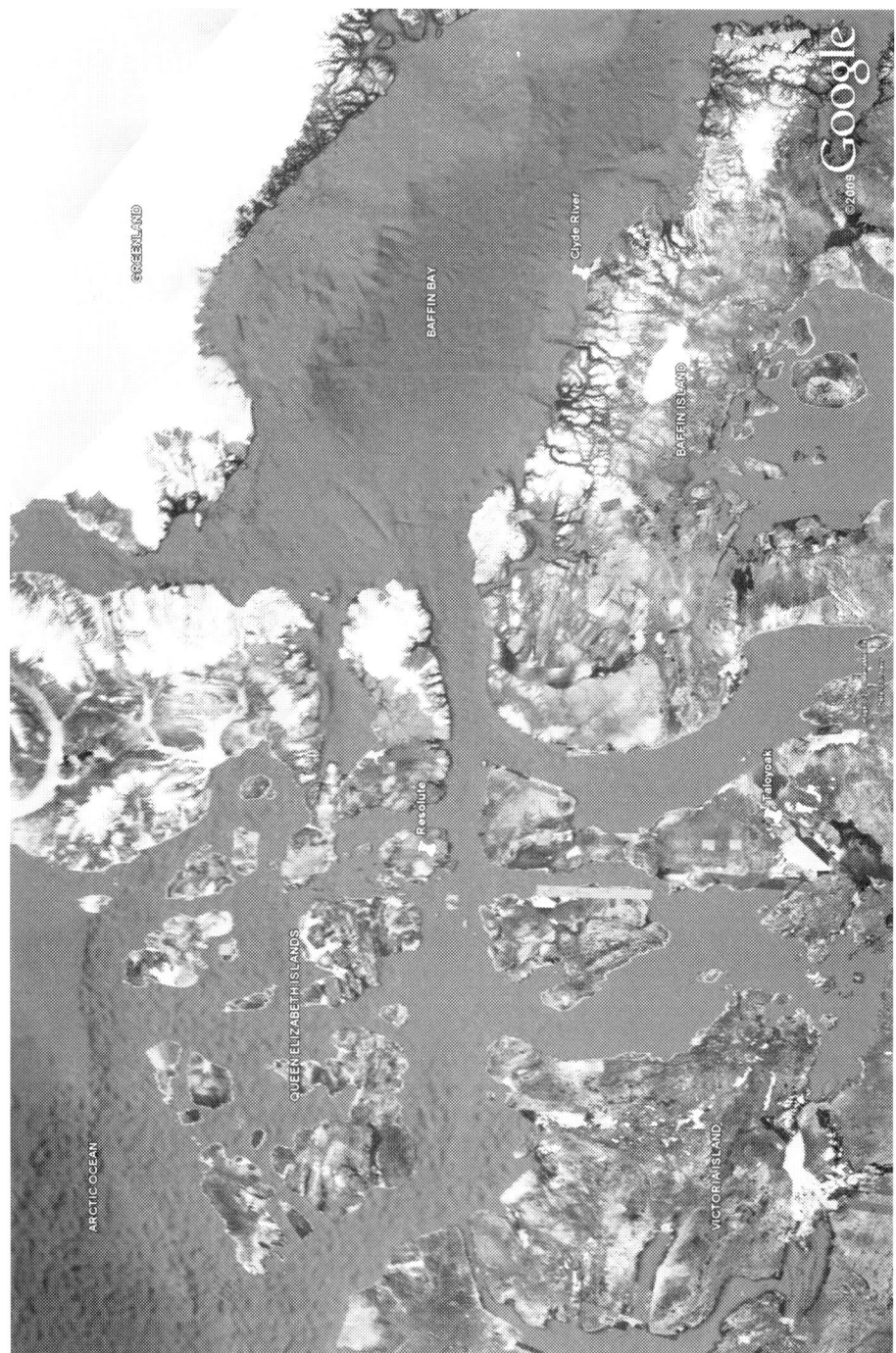

Figure 1. *Nunavut study sites. Map produced by J. Ferguson using GoogleEarth Pro (licence #1956742)*

Chapter One: *The Study Communities*

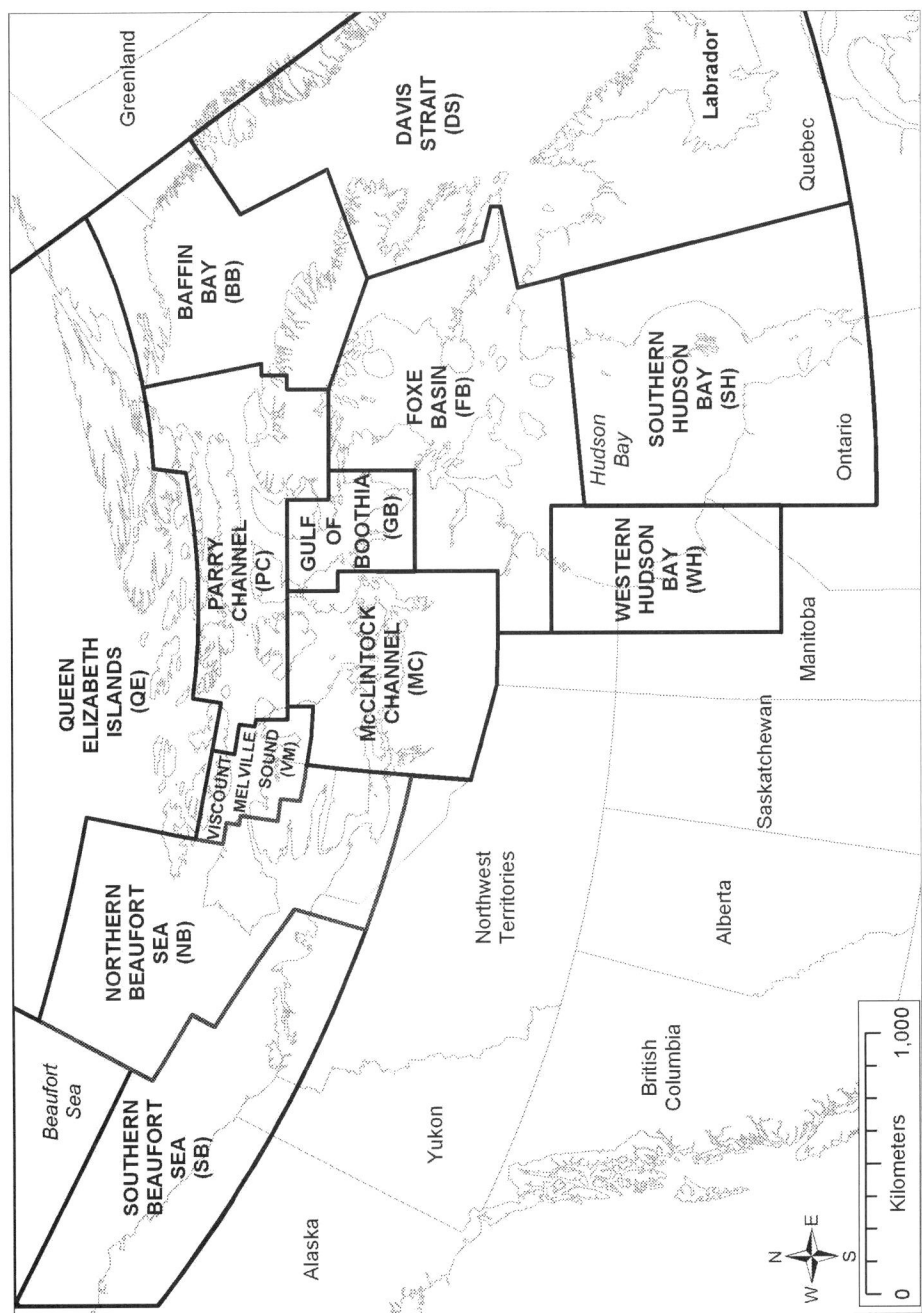

Figure 2. *Canadian polar bear population zones.*

Community Baseline Information

Clyde River, or *Kangirtugaapik*, is located on the east coast of Baffin Island (70°27'N, 68°38'W), about 750 km north-northwest from Iqaluit (Fig. 3). At the time of the polar bear sport-hunt research, the community was estimated to have an Inuit population of 785 (Nunavut Statistics 1999). However, the executive director of the Clyde River Housing Association (personal communication) stated that the unofficial, but likely more accurate, population count by Spring 2001, when fieldwork began in Clyde River was closer to 850. Based on an available labour force of 450 residents between 15 and 65 years of age, by the 'National Criteria' standard, 31.4% of Clyde Inuit were unemployed in 1999, as compared to the Nunavut-wide average of 20.7% (Nunavut Statistics 1999). The chief ethnological sources pertinent to Clyde River are by Foote (1967) and Wenzel (1981, 1991).

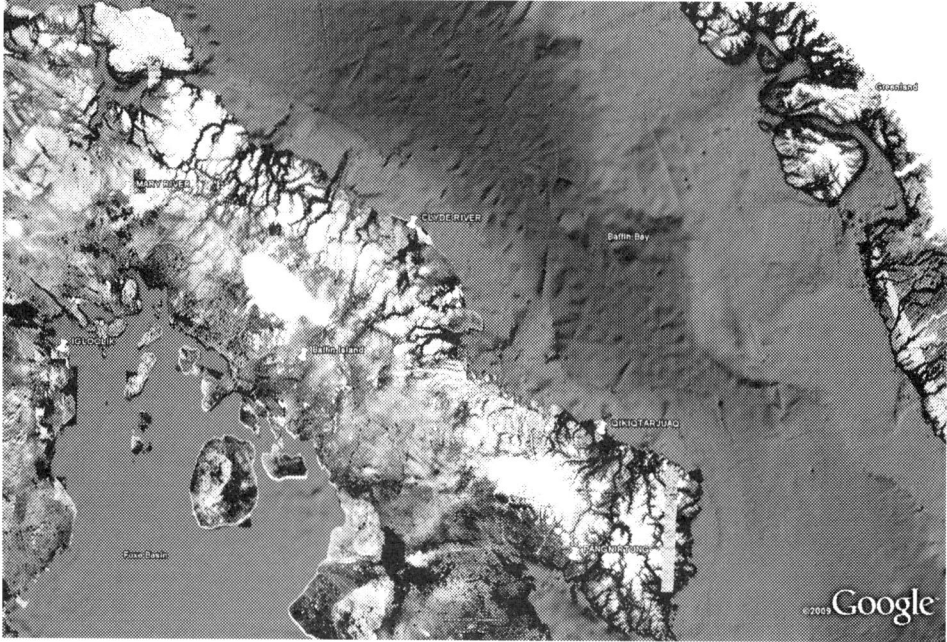

Figure 3. *Clyde River. Map produced by J. Ferguson using GoogleEarth Pro (licence #1956742)*

The main maritime area of importance to Clyde River hunters is Baffin Bay and associated fiords (Freeman 1975; Riewe 1991). The major polar bear population used by Clyde River Inuit is that of Baffin Bay, and this population is shared with Pond Inlet and Qikiqtaarjuak hunters.

Clyde River Inuit once ranged as far northward as Cape Adair and into Buchan Gulf for polar bear and to Cape Hooper and southern Home Bay to the south of the community (Fig. 3). However, following the substantial reduction in the community's polar bear quota from 45 to 20 animals in the mid-1980s (Davis 1999), most subsistence hunting of bear by Clyde River Inuit is now concentrated relatively close to the community, mainly between Eglinton Fiord and Henry Kater Peninsula. The 2000-2001 quota was 21 animals (14 males/7 females).

In 2001, Clyde River had three accredited outfitters. There were also seven active dogteams, all of whose owners did sport-hunt guiding (including two who also acted as outfitters). Additionally, two other men sometimes were hired to guide on polar bear hunts, but were not dogteam owners—when so hired, each borrowed a dogteam from a relative—and nine other men had received frequent work the preceding several years as the supply assistants on sport-hunts. Clyde's outfitters generally contract with southern-based sport-hunt wholesalers from Montréal (Quebec), Kamloops (British Columbia), and Toronto (Ontario) to book visiting polar bear trophy hunters.

Local regulation of polar bear hunting is through the Namautaq Hunter' and Trappers' Organization. As the number of Inuit hunters exceeds the number of available tags, the HTO operates the subsistence hunt using a community-wide lottery. However, decisions about sport hunting, involving both the percentage of the community quota available to the sport-hunt and the number of sport tags to each outfitter, are made through a general meeting of the HTO membership. In 2000-2001, ten of the twenty-one tags available to the community were distributed among the three sport-hunt outfitters for their clientele.

Clyde River, unlike either of the other study communities, not only has more than a single outfitter, but these outfitters receive their hunt clients from several southern expeditors. Among these expeditors are Joe Verni, located in Montréal, and Wes Vining of British Columbia. Prior to the current wholesaler-local outfitter arrangements, Namautaq HTO, under a contract with Jerome Knap's Canada North Expeditions, functioned as the sole outfitter in the community.

Resolute Bay lies at the southern tip of Cornwallis Island (74°41'N, 94°54'W) (Fig. 4). The 165 Inuit residents (Nunavut Statistics 2001) were moved from the island's original village site in 1975 to the present 'new community' location, approximately 8 km southwest of Resolute Bay's airport and the former Transport Canada base. There are five dogteams, all of whose owners are also polar bear sport-hunt guides, and one active hunt outfitter (who is also a dogteam owner and himself a guide). Resolute Bay, alone among the study communities in being accessible by commercial jet air service directly from southern Canada at the time of this research, has one of the lowest unemployment rates (10.2%) in Nunavut among residents 15 to 65 years of age (Nunavut Statistics 2001). While a considerable literature exists on the political history of the community, the main recent general reference on Resolute Bay Inuit land use and harvesting is Kemp *et al.* (1978).

Resolute Bay hunters pursue polar bears as far eastward as Radstock Bay, and sometimes Maxwell Bay on Devon Island, north into Wellington Channel and Queens Channel, and, to the south, off the east and west coast of Somerset Island in Prince Regent and Peel Sounds (Fig. 4) (*see* Riewe 1991). All of these locales are contained within the Lancaster Sound (formerly Parry Channel) bear population area (*see* Figs 2). During the 1980s, when outpost camps existed on Prince of Wales and Somerset Islands, Resolute Inuit ranged even farther south and west (Kemp *et al.* 1977), even to eastern Melville Island. Although Lancaster Sound polar bears are shared with hunters from Arctic Bay and Grise Fiord, the population area is so large that there is essentially no overlap in the hunting territories of the three communities.

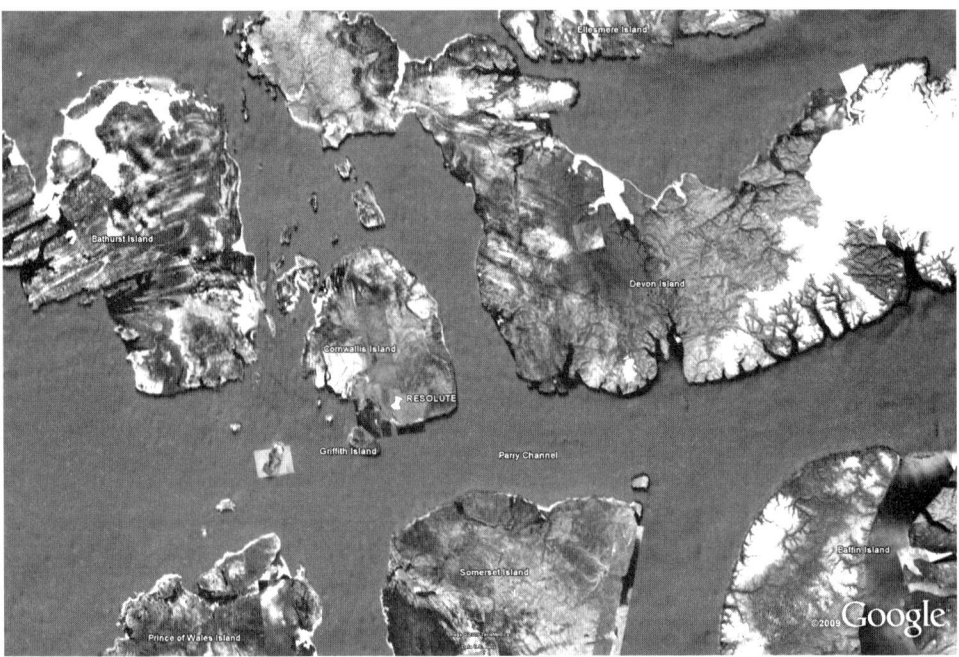

Figure 4. *Resolute Bay. Map produced by J. Ferguson using GoogleEarth Pro (licence #1956742)*

Among the Qikiqtaaluk region's 13 communities, Resolute has the highest polar bear quota (35 bears [24 males/11 females] in 2000-2001), and the second highest in Nunavut. In essence, at the time of this study, each Resolute household (n=34) could have potentially hunted a polar bear if tags were distributed directly to households.

The Hunters' and Trappers' Organization (HTO) executive committee oversees the allocation of each year's polar bear tags through a lottery system open to individuals who are members of the organization. It also designates the number of tags from this overall allocation that may be sold to the local outfitter for sport-hunt use, after which the outfitter then purchases up to 25 lottery-distributed tags from individual tag holders. Until 1998, the HTO was the main polar bear outfitter in Resolute. However, since then, a private outfitting firm, owned by Nathaniel Kulluk, receives all hunter clients coming to Resolute through a contract with Ontario-based Canada North Expeditions.

Taloyoak (formerly Spence Bay) lies on the southwest side of Boothia Peninsula, just above Boothia Isthmus (69°32'N, 93°32'W) (Fig. 5). The community is officially listed as having 720 Inuit residents (Nunavut Statistics 1999), but the Senior Administrative Officer placed the unofficial number as closer to 900 in May 2001 (personal communication). Unemployment at Taloyoak, in an available work force of 416 between the ages of 15 to 65, was 15.2% (Nunavut Statistics 1999). Scheduled air service to the community is available from Yellowknife, Northwest Territories to the West, and from the Nunavut communities of Rankin Inlet and Baker Lake to the south. Williamson (1977) and Riewe (1991) provide the best recent information on Taloyoak Inuit land and resource use.

Chapter One: *The Study Communities*

Figure 5. *Taloyoak. Map produced by J. Ferguson using GoogleEarth Pro (licence #1956742).*

Taloyoak in 2000-2001 had a community polar bear quota of 19 animals, which was divided between two population areas—M'Clintock Channel (12 bears: 8 Males/4 Females) and Gulf of Boothia (7 bears: 5M/2F). However, the community is not the sole harvester of bears in either area, sharing M'Clintock Channel with Gjoa Haven (2000 quota: 4 bears) and Cambridge Bay (2000 quota: also 4 bears) and the Gulf of Boothia population with Kugaaruk (2001 quota: 15 animals), Hall Beach (1), Iqloolik (7) and Repulse Bay (3).

Taloyoak's 2000-2001 overall quota of nineteen animals represented a significant decrease from the community's official base allocation of 27 bears through the 1990s (DSD 2001). This reduction had its genesis in the U.S. Fish and Wildlife Service imposing import sanctions under the 1972 *Marine Mammal Protection Act* (MMPA) on polar bear products, essentially hides, from the M'Clintock Channel area (*Nunatsiaq News* 2001). Since the MMPA prohibition, Nunavut's Department of Sustainable Development has imposed a moratorium on both subsistence and sport hunting of polar bears in M'Clintock Channel by all three communities (*Nunatsiaq News* 2001).

All aspects of polar bear hunting at Taloyoak are managed through the Hunters' and Trappers' Organization (HTO). By the HTO members' decision, until the 2000-2001 polar bear season, the community quota was divided between the Gulf of Boothia population area (7 bears) and M'Clintock Channel (12 animals). Taloyoak's use of the Gulf of Boothia was confined to subsistence hunting, while polar bear hunting in M'Clintock Channel was virtually reserved for sport hunters staging out of the community. In the 1999-2000 polar bear season, Taloyoak allocated ten tags for sport-hunts and only two for subsistence use.

Within the community, there are nine dogteams, although in the last year that the sport-hunt was held (Spring 2000), only six owners of teams sought the opportunity to guide a sport-hunter. The HTO executive committee makes decisions about the number of polar bear tags to allocate for sport hunting and the HTO acts as the local outfitter and hunt expeditor. Adventure Northwest Ltd., headquartered in Yellowknife, but with affiliation with Canada North Outfitting, was contracted as the southern advertiser and wholesaler of Taloyoak polar bear hunts.

Summary

It is worthy of note that, when this research commenced, the manner in which polar bear sport hunting was conducted varied from community to community. Clyde River, Resolute Bay, and Taloyoak differed significantly in how the allocation of part of the annual quota was made for sport hunting, in how trophy hunts were locally outfitted, and how guides and helpers were hired, and, perhaps most importantly, in how much control the community, either as a whole or through the local HTO, exerted over sport hunting.

On the other hand, the three communities shared at least two sport-hunt elements in common. These were a dependence on southern wholesalers for acquiring clients and at least a nominal role for the local HTO. Finally, it should also be noted that in each place (and, in fact, in any Nunavut community hosting sport hunting), the business component of the hunt, in contrast to the wildlife policy aspects, took place with virtually no Territorial Government assistance or oversight.

Chapter Two

POLAR BEARS AS A RESOURCE: AN OVERVIEW

Inuit Subsistence

No animal holds as visible or significant a place in Canadian Inuit culture as the polar bear (*Ursus maritimus*; Inuktitut: *nanuk*). This prominence is evidenced by the fact that, with Inuit, polar bear were the only other chief predator in the arctic marine environment, sharing that environment with man on virtually an equal basis, until the introduction of firearms. It is no surprise, therefore, that *nanuq* was a central figure in Inuit cosmology (*see* Boas 1888) and retains considerable symbolism for Inuit and non-Inuit today, albeit for very different reasons.

Inuit have hunted polar bears as an element of their ecological adaptation for millennia, with this hunting being conducted for spiritual-cultural reasons and to contribute to the traditional food economy (*see* Nelson 1969; Robbe 1975; Wenzel 1981). The contribution made by polar bears to the food economy of Nunavut Inuit is fairly well known (*see* Donaldson 1988; Wenzel 1991:82; Keith *et al.* 2005), but the degree to which *nanuk* retains ideological importance is much less understood (but *see* Sandell and Sandell 1996 regarding East Greenland).

Despite this last aspect remaining relatively unreported in the scientific literature, polar bear retain significance as a subsistence resource throughout Nunavut and other Inuit regions. However, as the Inuit subsistence environment has changed—from one defined by the application of knowledge and energy in the pursuit of food to one requiring a wider spectrum of resources, including money, in order to hunt—the subsistence role of polar bear in this system has also changed. Among the parameters of this new system are a very different spatial and demographic arrangement from but fifty years ago, the incorporation of Inuit into a 'globalized' political-economic situation, and the necessary assumption of obligations negotiated in the absence of Inuit.

In sum, *nanuk*, after nearly four millennia in which its cultural and economic importance was much as Boas recorded in 1888, today has assumed a role in the livelihoods of Inuit that may be larger than at any time in the past through the activity of outfitted sport hunting. This change is the product of a process that began for polar bears and Inuit around 1800 and which accelerated following the European Union's 1983 absolute ban on the import of Canadian sealskins and other seal products into any E.U. jurisdiction (Wenzel 1991). Thus, it is useful to review this evolution, albeit briefly, in order to historically locate the present iteration of the Inuit-bear relationship in the social and economic context of the Northwest Territories–Nunavut.

The Commoditization of Polar Bears *circa* 1850-1970

As European (and, later, American) interest in the Canadian Arctic moved beyond geographic exploration to the exploitation of its resources, this new focus eventually brought another dimension to the relationship between Inuit and polar bears. Through most of the 19th century, non-Inuit focused on the commercial exploitation of bowhead whales (*Balaena mysticetus*). However, after ca. 1890, as these large whales were reduced in numbers, other species—such as walrus and narwhal, both for their ivory—began to be hunted to supplement the diminishing revenue obtained from bowhead whale hunting. And polar bear, already sometimes killed for protection and recreation by the whalers, became part of this commerce. Indeed, as the profit margin of whaling fell, some ships' owners and captains sold places to huntsmen interested in shooting, among other game, polar bears for sport (*see* Ross 1985).

By the beginning of the last century, the bowhead populations of the Eastern Arctic had become so greatly reduced that furs and ivory not only supplanted whaling as foci of northern commerce, but also changed its nature. The crux of this change centered on the fact that, because Europeans were present in the North only in low numbers, efficient exploitation of these species could only be accomplished by Inuit, who already possessed the knowledge, skill, and energy to do so. Thus, a new economic dynamic emerged, the basis of which was the bartering of Inuit-produced furs and ivory for imported European goods including guns and ammunition, tea, molasses, cheap cloth and metal pots and tools.

Polar bears, while an element of this relationship, were for a considerable time only a minor item of trade, mainly because of the limitations of traditional Inuit technologies. However, by the 1940s, following the acquisition of more modern firearms by Inuit, polar bear clearly became more prominent in the northern fur trade. For example, fur records from the Hudson's Bay Company (HBC) post at Clyde River (Wenzel n.d.) show virtually no bear entries until 1943, the year after a weather station was established by the U.S. military adjacent to the HBC post. But, from that year forward, the annual HBC trade inventory included increasing numbers of polar bears, with as many as 55 being taken in trade at Clyde River by the mid-1960s.

While polar bear had at least by the 1940s become an item of some economic value in Inuit-European commerce, polar bear sport hunting, at least in any organized form, developed much more slowly. While it is undoubtedly the case that the Royal Canadian Mounted Police (RCMP), HBC employees and other non-Inuit may have hunted the occasional bear, there is no evidence of recreational hunting being conducted in any organized fashion in these years.

Again, unpublished records (RCMP 1969) from Clyde River are useful-referring to only one 'sport-hunt' as occurring between 1955 and 1970 and that by an American military officer visiting the nearby U.S. Coast Guard station at Cape Christian. Moreover, from 1969 (the year of the aforementioned hunt), until 1983, it would appear that only four polar bear sport-hunts (DSD 2001) occurred in the whole of the Baffin Bay polar bear population region (*see* Fig. 2).

Department of Sustainable Development archival data (DSD 2001) indicate a similar situation regarding recreational hunting for polar bear in the Lancaster Sound area, noting only one contracted hunt before the 1980s. But it also appears that government biologists as early as 1966 were considering the potential economic benefits of a sport-hunt for polar bear, at least a limited way, to Inuit communities (National Archive of Canada. RG109. V.19. WLT200-5).

It must also be mentioned that prior to 1969-70, when a quota-tag system was introduced as a formal aspect of polar management (*see* Lentfer 1974), only HBC, RCMP and fur auction records provide a general means for tracking polar bear harvesting by

Inuit and others. Thus, statements about polar bear hunting before ca. 1970, especially as organized recreation, should be viewed as needing further examination.

The Business of Polar Bear Sport Hunting: 1970-1985

Between roughly the mid-1960s and the mid-1980s, several events relevant to Inuit polar bear hunting, as a specific activity and as an element within the wider framework of the then northern subsistence system, took place. The first of these, focused on the biological conservation of polar bears, was politico-legal in its nature, and remains in force today.

In 1973, after more than five years of extensive discussions, Canada, Norway, Denmark and the United States, joined by the then Soviet Union the following year, signed the *Agreement on Conservation of Polar Bears* (ACPB) (Lentfer 1974) which, in 1981, was made permanent by the signatories (Fikkan *et al.* 1993). Canada, like the other signatories of the agreement, assumed shared management of polar bear for conservation and sustainable use.

But Canada also recognized that it had an obligation to balance these conservation goals with the socioeconomic and cultural needs of its Inuit citizens, most especially those living in the Northwest Territories (NWT). Among signing nations, only Canadian Inuit were provided with subsistence access to bears, through an annual quota of about 440 polar bears (*see* Table 1), and the right to assign a part of this quota for profit to non-Inuit sport hunters. In contrast, Inuit–Iñupiaq hunters in Greenland and Alaska were only permitted to bear hunt for subsistence (IUCN 1985).

This early quota system was based on historic, mainly HBC, records of polar bear hides traded at various locations over the last 5 years of harvest (from trade information) that was used to obtain an 'average harvest' for each community. This average number was the initial quota, or the established maximum harvest level for each of the Inuit communities in the then Northwest Territories. Any community with an approved local quota was, in turn, free to allocate a portion of its quota for sale to sport hunters. However, as will be discussed, sport hunting activity by non-resident hunters was almost non-existent in the NWT during this period.

The ACPB, and its associated quota, was at most a partial effector of the changing relationship between Inuit and polar bears. At least as important were specific spatio-demographic and economic changes that occurred during this time.

By about 1965, following the near-complete centralization of local Inuit populations into regional centers, hunters found their spatial relationship to traditional resources considerably altered. One outcome of this changed pattern of settlement in relation to resources was that Inuit began to incorporate increasingly expensive imported tools into their hunting inventory. The most notable of these, and the most noticed and remarked on, was the snowmobile.

Beginning in the mid-1960s, the snowmobile, or Ski-Doo, first became available through the Hudson's Bay Company in Eastern Arctic communities. It almost immediately began to displace dogteams as the preferred winter mode of transport for both terrestrial and marine hunting (*see* Jorgensen 1990 and Wenzel 1991 regarding this transition in, respectively, North Alaska and the Eastern Canadian Arctic).

The rapidity of the sweep of this technological change in less than a decade, roughly from the late 1960s to early 1970s, is illustrated by data collected from Clyde River and Resolute Bay during this time. At Clyde River, the first Inuit-owned snowmobile appeared in 1964 and seven years later all but 10 of the 42 hunters in the community had mechanized, and, by 1980, no Clyde hunter was dependent on dogs (Wenzel 1991). Similarly, by 1976, there was just one active dogteam in the Resolute Bay area and this was at the distant outpost camp of Kuganiuk, located at Creswell Bay, Somerset Island (Kemp *et al.* 1978)

Table 1: Northwest Territories Community Polar Bear Quotas—1973[1]

Settlement	Quota	Zone[2]
Tuktoyaktuk	14	24
Paulatuk	11	25
Coppermine[3]	2	26
Bathurst Inlet	1	27
Cambridge Bay	10	29
Holman Island	12	
Sachs Harbour	18	30
Grise Fiord	27	31
Resolute Bay	34	
Pond Inlet	13	32
Arctic Bay	12	
Cape Christian[4]	42[5]	
Pangnirtung	8	
Frobisher Bay[3]	12	
Lake Harbour[3]	7	
Broughton Island[3]	16	
Cape Dorset	6	
Port Burwell[4]	8	
Gjoa Haven	8	33
Igloolik	16	
Hall Beach	7	
Pelly Bay	10	
Repulse Bay	16	
Spence Bay[3]	22	
Rankin Inlet	8	34
Eskimo Point[3]	10	
Whale Cove	7	
Chesterfield Inlet	5	
Southampton Island[3]	65	35
Belcher Islands[3]	15	37
TOTAL QUOTA	**442**	

[1] In 1973, the Northwest Territories included all of what is now Nunavut and the Inuvialuit Settlement Area of the present NWT.

[2] Designated polar bear administrative sub-divisions; community activities frequently overlapped these zones.

[3] These communities are now, respectively, Kugluktuk, Iqaluit, Kimmirut, Qikiqtarjuak, Taloyoak, Salliq, and Sanikiluaq.

[4] Cape Christian and Port Burwell no longer exist as administrative or habitation sites; after 1976, the Cape Christian designation was changed to Clyde River.

[5] Clyde River's annual quota was increased to 45 animals ca.1976 and remained at that number until ca.1986.

The changed spatial pattern of Nunavut hunters now living in permanent settlements, *vis-à-vis* their wildlife base made the snowmobile and other new modes of transportation, such as outboard motor-equipped freighter canoes, critically important for hunter mobility. It also required hunters to be able to acquire the significant sums of money needed to purchase this equipment. Indeed, in no small sense, money, itself, became a subsistence factor. Along with this costly expansion of an Inuk hunter's basic tool kit, two other changes, one substantial and the second initially less so, enlarged the subsistence role of polar bear for Inuit and laid the ground for further commoditization of the species.

The most important of these was that by the mid-1960s, formerly undervalued northern products, like raw sealskins and polar bear hides, became more attractive, albeit briefly, to external markets. The primary example is sealskins. Ringed seal, always an important food species for most Inuit, took on a new importance after 1963 as a commercial market developed for seal pelts in Europe. From a pre-1963 situation in which ringed sealskins brought $0.50 to $1.00 from the HBC, prices grew during the heyday of the sealskin trade to nearly $22 by 1980 (*see* Jelliss 1978).

A similar market-price trend affected the value of polar bear, especially around the mid-1970s (Smith and Jonkel 1975a, b; Smith and Stirling 1976). At the start of the 1970s, hides typically were purchased at $35-$50 per linear foot (Anonymous 1972). By 1975, however, at the height of overseas demand from Japan and, to a lesser degree, (West) Germany, polar bear hides sometimes commanded as much as $200.00 per linear foot (Wenzel n.d.) and trade became an increasingly important aspect of polar bear hunting. However, by 1980, the auction price of a polar bear stabilized at about half the mid-1970s level (generally $75-$100 per linear foot, depending on a hide's condition and at what time during the year it was traded).

Non-Inuit interest in furs that formerly had found only a limited, if any, market provided Inuit with access to much of the money hunters needed to obtain and operate the new equipment that, after the creation of permanent settlements, had become important to efficient harvesting. Thus, where the average revenue earned by Clyde River hunters from combined seal and polar bear sales ca. 1972 was slightly less than $1,400.00, in 1980 this combined average was almost $2,500, or about an 80 per cent increase (Wenzel 1991). Moreover, those few hunters who enjoyed multiple polar bear kills in a year (several had two and two men had three) earned as much as $4,000-6,000 (Wenzel n.d.).

However, as, first, polar bear prices began their decline in the late 1970s to the more modest levels paid earlier in the decade and, second, in 1982-83, the market for sealskins collapsed, Inuit were caught in a precarious resource situation. (At about this time, the sale of raw narwhal ivory also came under temporary market embargo [Harper 1984].) Inuit still remained in established communities distant from most important food resources and, thus, still technologically dependent for consistent access to these resources. However, with the loss of external markets for their formerly most valuable wild exports, a hunter's ability to obtain the money required for needed equipment through the sale of byproducts from food hunting (sealskins, narwhal ivory) was considerably weakened. Finally, this condition was at least somewhat affected by the fact that the ACPB quota meant that Inuit could not increase the size of the polar bear harvest to compensate for the depressed prices received for polar bear hides.

The Contemporary Sport-Hunt: 1985-2000

The fact that the ACPB, from its beginning, included a sport-hunt proviso for Canadian Inuit (a 'Native-guided polar bear sport-hunt' [Fikkan *et al.* 1993:100]) suggests that some interest existed in such an activity as early as the mid-1970s. However, as the data (DSD 2001) that are available show, polar bear sport hunting appears to have developed only slowly during the 1970s in several (but not all) areas of the NWT and, it was far from extensive even in the early 1980s. As such, sport hunting typically accounted for only a few animals in each region relative to the local quotas.

Rather, what these data (Table 2) indicate is that Inuit participation in sport hunting, except in a few communities, was minimal. Also shown is that significant growth in the sport-hunt began in 1982-83 and correlates almost exactly with the collapse of the sealskin economy across the NWT.

By the mid-1980s, non-Inuit hunting of polar bear began to take on increasing significance, both as a percentage of the quotas allotted to communities and in economic terms. This increase, occurring shortly after the near total collapse of the world sealskin market, suggests that sport hunting was a response to the economic impact of that event on Inuit subsistence hunters, rather than simply a desire on the part of Inuit to suddenly 'go commercial.'

To understand this, it is useful to ask why the most monetarily rational use of local polar bear quotas, or at least part of these quotas as used today by communities, did not emerge before the mid-1980s. Again, a number of factors appear to have influenced this change.

The most direct factor is that before the mid-1980s few of the communities in the Eastern or Central Arctic regions of the NWT were reliably accessible via scheduled air service. As a result, it was virtually impossible for sport hunters (and other visitors) to travel to and from communities with some expectation of regularity. Government of Nunavut data (DSD 2001) show the one exception before the early to mid-1980s was the Mackenzie Delta–Beaufort Sea region of the then hyphenated Northwest Territories. Here, expectations of an oil and gas economic boom prompted improved transportation services throughout the area before many other parts of the Territories.

These same data (*see* Table 3) show that it was in this region that polar bear sport hunting developed earliest and that the hunt has maintained some constancy and continuity. In contrast, sport polar bear hunting developed more slowly and, in a few Eastern and Central Arctic locales, only rather recently.

The most important action affecting the growth of polar bear sport hunting in Nunavut-Northwest Territories, especially in the Qikiqtaaluk and Kitikmeot regions, came in the late 1980s. The collapse of the sealskin sector of the subsistence economy, coupled with the interruption of narwhal ivory sales, severely disrupted the flow of monetary income available to hunters from wildlife products. In an effort to alleviate the negative economic impact of the European trade ban, Territorial authorities identified tourism, to include sport hunting and fishing, as one mechanism for providing non-wage sector income, and thus enhance local community economic development.

Chapter Two: *Polar Bears as a Resource*

Table 2: Annual Quota (AQ) and Sport Harvest (SH), 1970-2000 (DSD 2001)

Year	Number of Communities	AQ	SH	SH as % of AQ
1970	30	442	4	0.9
1971	29	"	?	0.0
1972	"	"	7	1.5
1973	"	"	5	1.1
1974	"	"	3	0.6
1975	"	"	0	0.0
1976	"	445[1]	5	1.1
1977	"	"	3	0.7
1978	"	"	6	1.3
1979	"	"	4	0.9
10YR Subtotal	29	4432	37	0.8
1980	"	445	3	0.7
1981	"	"	7	1.5
1982	"	"	17	3.8
1983	"	"	22	4.9
1984	"	"	32	7.2
1985	"	"	22	4.9
1986	"	427[2]	38	9.0
1987	"	"	56	13.1
1988	"	"	54	12.6
1989	"	"	56	13.1
10YR Subtotal	29	4418	307	7.1
1990	"	427[3]	44	10.3
1991	"	"	50	11.7
1992	"	"	34	7.9
1993	"	"	32	7.5
1994	"	"	49	11.5
1995	"	"	86	20.1
1996	"	"	84	19.7
1997	"	"	92	21.5
1998	25[4]	400	63	15.7
1999	"	"	75	18.7
2000	"	"	65	16.2
90-00 Subtotal	25	4616	674	14.6
31 YR TOTAL	------	13,466	1,018	7.6

[1] Circa 1976, the annual quota at Clyde River was raised from 42 to 45 animals.

[2] In 1986, the annual quota at Clyde River was reduced from 45 to 21 bears and that of Qikiqtarjuak (formerly Broughton Island) was raised from 16 to 21 bears (*see* Davis 1999).

[3] From about 1990, Territorial authorities responsible for polar bear management instituted a 'flexible quota system'; in the absence of exact annual quota information for each community, the annual figure(s) provided should be viewed as being of the 'best guess' variety.

[4] In 1999, the annual quotas (*see* Table 1) of Tuktoyaktuk, Paulatuk, Holman Island and Sachs Harbour were transferred from Nunavut to the NWT, with a consequent reduction of 27 animals in Nunavut's quota.

As part of a tourism development strategy, several programs were developed by the NWT Department of Economic Development and Tourism (ED&T) for the training and certification of Inuit as guides, followed by one to develop community-based outfitters—programs that were even incorporated, albeit briefly, into the curriculum of Arctic College. In addition, the Territorial Government, through ED&T, and Inuit business organizations like Nunasi Corporation (the economic development arm of the Tungavik Federation of Nunavut), provided start-up funding for local sport-hunt entrepreneurs. Finally, and perhaps most important with regard to the shape of the industry as it functions in Nunavut today, contacts with southern big game hunt wholesalers expanded.

As potentially attractive economically as sport hunting appeared, its development, even after the sealskin price crash, was slow. At Clyde River, intense community discussion was conducted for nearly two years before a majority of the Hunters' and Trappers' Organization members agreed to allocate two of Clyde's annual quota of 21 bears to visiting sport-hunters (*see* Davis 1999). While such reticence was not necessarily the case in every community, it does underscore how deliberate was the decision by Inuit in some communities to accept sport hunting. In fact, it was found during the course of the research, that at least a small number of Inuit still object to sport hunting, as will be discussed later in this volume.

While government programs, local economic necessity and progressive improvements in air transportation to Nunavut communities all have been important to the growth of the polar bear sport hunting industry in the North and in the South, the satisfaction visiting hunters experience in obtaining trophies is also critical. The fact that a German, Mexican, or American hunter may pay upward of US$20,000.00 in itself implies that the probability of hunting success must be high. As Table 4 shows, success has been the norm and, in light of the cost of a polar bear hunt, it is not surprising that those communities and areas where great success has been realized attract a steady flow of sport hunters.

In addition, the perception of what is a 'trophy' is also an important (*see* Jones 1999), if less predictable, element in the ability of a community or area to attract clients. Interviews with southern hunters who have pursued polar bear in Nunavut or the Northwest Territories make it clear that at one level a polar bear, because of its rarity of place in the average sport-hunter's display room, meets the meaning of the term. As several sport-hunters noted during their interviews, only one in 1,000 trophy rooms has a polar bear—typically as a full body, rather than rug, mount.

However, size is also a factor in determining what is considered a trophy, with larger, especially male, animals being the most desired. Thus, communities (and wholesalers) whose customers report harvesting larger male animals are favoured. This is illustrated by two hunts that took place from Clyde River in the 1990s.

In 1992, an American hunter bagged a 3.4m (11 foot, 2 inch) male bear. The following year more than a hundred sportsmen requested Clyde as their preferred hunt destination according to the wholesaler then booking clients for the community (Canada North Outfitting, Personal Communication).

Chapter Two: *Polar Bears as a Resource*

Table 3: NWT–Nunavut Polar Bear Population Area[1] and Sport-Hunts, 1970-2000

Year	Population Area, Annual Quota & Sport Harvest [2,3]										
	SH [15]	WH [25]	MC [43]	DS [35]	BB [58]	LS[4] [86]	FB [115]	SB [25]	NB [30]	GB [10]	VM ?
1970						1			3		
1971											
1972									7		
1973					3				2		
1974					1				2		
1975											
1976									5		
1977								1	2		
1978								1	4		1
1979									4		
1970-1979 =37					4	1			7	24	1
1980				1					2		
1981				4			1		2		
1982				5		4	1		4		3
1983					1	4	2		8		7
1984				6	4	8		1	6		7
1985				6	1	10		1	3		1
1986[6]				5	2	15	4	1	8		3
1987				6	2	19	4	3	9	2	11
1988				4	4	15	8	1	8	3	11
1989				7	2	18	7	3	8	2	9
1980-1989 =307				44	16	93	27	10	58	7	52
1990				7	3	18	4	1	5	2	4
1991			2	3	2	24	7	1	2	1	8
1992				7		21	1	1	3	1	
1993				4		20	4		1	3	
1994				5		25	7	3	2		7
1995		5	3	9		27	11	14	12	5	
1996		8	7	15		28	3	9	8	6	
1997	2	16		8		28	3	19	12	4	
1998	3	12		6		27		7	3	5	
1999	2	9		7		28	3	16	6	4	
2000		13	2	12		28	2			4	4
1990-2000 =674	7	65	22	78		274	45	71	54	42	16
TOTAL =1,018	7	65	66	99		368	82	88	145	49	69

[1] Area designations are those presently used to distinguish polar bear population groupings: respectively, Southern Hudson Bay, Western Hudson Bay, M'Clintock Channel, Davis Strait, Baffin Bay, Lancaster Sound, Foxe Basin, Southern Beaufort Sea, Northern Beaufort Sea, Gulf of Boothia and Viscount Melville Sound (*see also* Fig. 2). (N.B. The polar bear zones shown in Table 1 are in some cases now divided into several population areas [i.e., Zone 32, formerly all of Baffin Island, is now divided between Areas BB, FB, DS and LS].)

[2] Annual area quotas have been derived from the sum of the quotas of communities hunting each area.

[3] Population areas show considerable variation in annual level of sport-hunt activity; such change may relate to the 'flexible quota' system adopted for management and conservation in the 1990s, or because the biological data suggested a need to reduce or stop harvesting.

[4] Subsumed here under Lancaster Sound are the Norwegian Bay and Kane Basin areas, both of which are used exclusively by Grise Fiord hunters.

Table 4: Success Rate for Polar Bear Sport-Hunts in Four Canadian Population Areas (Source: DSD 2001)

YEAR	LANCASTER SOUND	M'CLINTOCK CHANEL	W. HUDSON BAY	SOUTH BEAUFORT SEA
1993/94	89%//25 of 28	No Sport Hunt	No Sport Hunt	50%//3 of 6
1994/95	87%//27 of 31	71%//5 of 7	No Sport Hunt	74%//14 of 19
1995/96	87%//28 of 32	73%//8/of 11	No Sport Hunt	43%//9 of 21
1996/97	96%//28 of 29	100%//16 of 16	No Sport Hunt	73%//19 of 26
1997/98	93%//26 of 28	75%//12 of 16	100%//2 of 2	50%//7 of 14
1998/99	87%//28 of 32	56%//9 of 16	100%//3 of 3	84%//16 of 19
1999/00	93%//29 of 31	93%//13 of 14	100%//2 of 2	89%//8 of 9

By comparison, in 1995, three American hunters completed successful hunts undertaken from Clyde River with bears in the 2.3m (7.5 feet) to 2.75m (9 foot) range. The hunter with the smallest of the bears on several occasions took the author aside to inquire whether his was a 'good' bear. Indeed, a frequent complaint by Inuit who guide sport-hunters is that their clients will, on numerous occasions, show no desire to hunt particular animals because they are 'too small.'

Aside from these positives, one factor has had a negative effect on the polar bear sport-hunt industry. This is the United States' *Marine Mammal Protection Act* (MMPA). The MMPA, like the *Endangered Species Act*, dates from the early 1970s. However, unlike the *Endangered Species Act*, it is applied only to marine mammals, and generally without regard to the actual risk to a species.

In general terms, the MMPA prohibits the importation of virtually all raw and processed items from seals, whales and other marine mammals, the last including polar bear. As such, the *Act* bars importation into the U.S. of polar bear products in all forms, whether as raw or tanned whole hides, teeth and claws (even when incorporated into items of jewelry or art), the meat, or any manufactured part of the animal, including the hair (once popular for dressing salmon and trout flies). However, the MMPA's polar bear restriction also contained provisions of importance to Nunavut's sport-hunt—namely, exemptions for certain populations of bears (*see* Table 5) for which biological data show that limited hunting is sustainable.

Although polar bear are not officially considered as being endangered, not least because of the conservation effect of the international *Agreement on the Conservation of Polar Bears*, the MMPA has affected the sport-hunt industry. This is because uncertainties exist about the reliability of the data pertaining to the biological sustainability of some polar bear populations. When the U.S. Fish and Wildlife Service has concerns about a Canadian polar bear population, it can, under the MMPA, block the import of polar bear trophies taken from any population for which uncertainty exists until data persuasive of sustainability are obtained. As will be discussed, this is exactly what occurred in the case of the Taloyoak sport-hunt in M'Clintock Channel (the hunts from Gjoa Haven and Cambridge Bay in this area were similarly affected). Indeed, the 'unlucky' 1995 Clyde hunter referred to earlier, and his two more successful colleagues, were still waiting in 2002 to import their Clyde River trophies because of US F&W doubts about the Baffin Bay polar bear population data.

Table 5: Current[1] MMPA Import Status of Nunavut–NWT[2] Polar Bear Populations[3]

Approved Populations	User Communities
Lancaster Sound	Arctic Bay, Grise Fiord, Resolute Bay
Northern Beaufort Sea	Holman,[4] Paulatuk, Sachs Harbour, Kugluktuk
Norwegian Bay	Grise Fiord
Southern Beaufort Sea	Aklavik, Inuvik, Paulatuk, Tuktoyaktuk
Viscount Melville Sound	Cambridge Bay, Holman
West Hudson Bay	Arviat, Baker Lake, Chesterfield Inlet, Rankin Inlet, Whale Cove
Blocked Populations	**User Communities**
Baffin Bay	Qikiqtaarjuak, Clyde River, Pond Inlet
Kane Basin	Grise Fiord
Davis Strait	Iqaluit, Pangnirtung,[5] Kimmirut
Foxe Basin	Cape Dorset, Igloolik, Kimmirut, Repulse Bay, Hall Beach, Chesterfield Inlet
South Hudson Bay	Sanikiluaq
M'Clintock Channel	Taloyoak, Gjoa Haven, Cambridge Bay
Gulf of Boothia	Taloyoak, Kugaaruk, Igloolik, Hall Beach, Repulse Bay

[1] Aklavik, Holman, Sachs Harbour, Inuvik and Paulatuk are within the political jurisdiction of the Northwest Territories.

[2] Aklavik, Holman, Sachs Harbour, Inuvik and Paulatuk are within the political jurisdiction of the Northwest Territories.

[3] MMPA 'listing' of a population does not prohibit polar bear hunting by Americans or other sportsmen, only the importation into the U.S. of hides or other items from these prohibited populations. Listing may occur because biological data suggests that a population in under harvesting stress or because reasonable data are unavailable (i.e., as is the case re. Greenland subsistence use of Baffin Bay and Kane Basin polar bears).

[4] The current name for 'Holman' is 'Ulukhaktok.'

[5] The current name for 'Pangnirtung' is 'Pangnirtuuq.'

Such extra-territorial concerns can have serious consequences for a community's sport-hunt, as the majority of the hunt clientele that travels to Nunavut seeking trophy polar bears are from the United States. For instance, Clyde River no longer receives requests for bookings from American sportsmen, despite a continuing reputation for large bears. Thus, the MMPA listing can impede what has become an important element in the maintenance of subsistence activities by some hunters and to the larger economic development potential the hunt affords communities engaged in sport hunting activities.

Summary

The situation in Nunavut at the time of this research was that polar bear sport hunting offered the opportunity for individual Inuit and communities to obtain considerably larger sums of scarce money than was otherwise possible through the more traditional sale of furs. As a business, the sport-hunt was fairly recent in its development, having been affected by earlier logistic difficulties and by a reticence on the part of Inuit to participate in its development. Since 1985, improvements in the North's transportation and accommodation infrastructure have allowed non-Inuit relatively easy access to Nunavut communities.

More relevant to the emergence of sport hunting as an industry, however, was the impact of the European Union sealskin boycott, the impact of which is still deeply felt on the monetary well-being of Inuit living and working outside the wage sector of the economy. This event precipitated both a government strategy of economic development and a cultural acceptance by Inuit of what was seen by them to be a highly non-traditional, albeit utilitarian, use of polar bear.

The reality of the Nunavut sport-hunt today is that, for some Inuit, and especially those for whom wildlife harvesting is an occupation, the income provided through guiding visitor-hunters is an important, and for some an essential, subsistence resource. For others, it is a business, one of the few that can be indigenous to Nunavummiut. It is also one that, as the examples from Clyde River and Taloyoak demonstrate, can be very unreliable. However, underlying the economic possibilities and political problems surrounding the contemporary sport-hunt is the fact that polar bear very much remain a cultural resource for all Inuit.

Chapter Three

INUIT TEK AND THE SPORT-HUNT

Traditional Ecological Knowledge (TEK)

As Usher (2000) has pointed out, Traditional Ecological Knowledge (also known as Local, Indigenous or Traditional Knowledge, and specifically in Nunavut as *Inuit Qaujimajatuqangit*)—i.e., the information about animals, the local ecology and the overall operations of the ecosystem that Inuit or other peoples have acquired through personal experience and intergenerational transfer of knowledge—comprises several levels or strata. These range from specific facts about environmental characteristics, such as the quality of the snow (important, e.g., for snowhouse construction), and of animal behaviour, through the interrelationship between the physical and biological elements of the environment that may comprise good seal habitat, to beliefs about how human actions and even thoughts and speech affect animals and the outcome of the hunt.

That the knowledge that Inuit have acquired through generations of close observation and interaction with polar bears has practical and cultural importance is almost too obvious to state. Further, that the traditional knowledge that Inuit possess about their general environment and of polar bear, in particular, is a critical factor in the subsistence use of the species is also understood. But, whether Inuit hunt polar bear for subsistence or to facilitate sports hunters' pursuit of trophy bears, the fundamental knowledge that only Inuit possess about the behavior of *nanuk* and the environment is critical to both a successful hunt and, sometimes, survival of the hunter. After all, no matter how well they may be equipped, the visitor-hunters who come to Nunavut lack experience with polar bear and the Arctic environment.

TEK in the Present Research

While Inuit traditional knowledge about polar bear is culturally rich and pragmatically detailed, the tendency in TEK-related research, especially in the social sciences, has been to focus on the cognitive component of this knowledge. It is only recently that TEK's potential for deriving ecological insights about polar bear (*see*, for instance, Atatahak and Banci 2001) and other species began to be appreciated.

The aspect of TEK examined in the present research was undertaken to better understand one facet of the most basic kind of information present in Inuit knowledge of polar bear. This is, what cues do Inuit use to discriminate male from female bears before their capture.

Inclusion of TEK, as an aspect of this project, was limited for two reasons. First, a truly comprehensive TEK study, providing insight into all the levels of traditional knowledge noted by Usher, would require a dedicated research effort well beyond the resources and objectives of this project. It would, in fact, be a study of *Inuit Qaujimajatuqangit*, or IQ (*see* Wenzel 2004 for a discussion of *Inuit Qaujimajatuqangit*).

The second reason was that the interest here is in those aspects of traditional ecological knowledge that are most relevant to the project objectives. Because of these objectives, it became apparent that no 'item' of Inuit ecological knowledge about polar bear had greater importance, given the present regulatory climate governing the harvesting of the species, than the ability to discriminate between male and female animals. In addition, within the complex traditional knowledge inventory about polar bears held by Inuit, no aspect of TEK has more critical implications for using the sport-hunt as both a conservation tool and as a means of furthering Inuit subsistence interests. The explanation of the critical nature of such a seemingly ordinary aspect of polar bear TEK requires a brief look at the systematic management of polar bear that came into effect in the Northwest Territories in 1968 and which, with one critical modification, regulates Inuit use of the species in Nunavut today.

The Management System

In 1968, Canadian polar bear harvesting, which includes both subsistence and sport hunting, came under formal regulation, the core feature of which was, and remains today, the setting of an annual quota (Fikkan *et al.* 1993). The essence of this management program was that it set a ceiling on the total number of animals that may be taken in a year. Furthermore, within the Northwest Territories (and now, also Nunavut), this overall allowable quota was sub-divided into community quotas, based on the perceived historic annual harvest of polar bears by Inuit in each community.

The first territorial and community quotas were set using the average number of bears harvested (or, more accurately, traded) during the several years prior to 1968 (Mulrennan 1997). In essence, this number represented a maximum ceiling above which no more bears could be captured in a year. In fact, 'The Quota' became, from both a community and individual hunter's perspective, the main feature affecting access to the species and was generally, along with the restriction on harvesting cubs, the most issues-based element of the management system (Wenzel n.d.).

First set at approximately 440 animals per annum for the whole of the N.W.T., communities received allocations ranging from as few as five at Chesterfield Inlet to as many as sixty-five bears at Salliq (formerly Coral Harbour) within this overall maximum. Further, while any community quota could be modified because of new biological data or regulatory violations, such as harvesting restricted animals (nursing females and/or cubs), in most communities the original allocation resulted in a fixed ceiling, automatically renewed annually. Even when there were instances of violations, the penalty was almost always temporary, affecting only the next hunting year.

The overall Northwest Territories quota, and that of most communities, experienced relatively little change until the mid-1980s (*see* Davis 1999, regarding Clyde River and Qikiqtarjuak). In 1992-1993, the management system, in terms of the feature that most affected communities—the annual quota— underwent a very significant modification. This was to establish local quotas using a population dynamics-based approach toward polar bears and was introduced in order to better manage for biological sustainability. As such, for the first time, science became a significant component in polar bear management. Its main element was to shift the community-level regulatory tool from a fixed ceiling for the annual polar bear catch to a 'flexible quota' based on certain attributes of the preceding year's harvest. As a result, a community's annual quota could be adjusted in response to actual results from the previous year's hunting.

TEK and Polar Bear Conservation

The essential element of this change in approach was that, while communities continued to receive an annual allocation, this represented a base that was no longer simply composed of all the polar bears that were 'legal.' Rather, the revamped quota system, while initially set for most communities at the levels already established 'historically' (which, in fact, rested on HBC trade records and thus did not necessarily accurately reflect total captures in any year), now also included within its design a variable that had not been present in the old system, namely 'sub-quotas' within each community's, and region's, overall quota; that is, recommended levels of harvesting for male and female bears. This factor was introduced in order to more effectively manage for the long-term biological sustainability of the various bear populations in Nunavut through more discriminating harvesting. It also meant that it was now important not only for each community to contain its harvest within its assigned base annual quota, but also to harvest in a more targeted way.

The new harvest standard became one in which a minimum harvest ratio of two male bears to every female is maintained. As a result, a community's annual allocation was no longer dependent on simply avoiding an outright overkill of its base quota or the killing of prohibited bears—for instance, females with cubs. Rather, it was maintenance of a least this basic ratio of male to female animals that was critical if a community was to avoid downward adjustment of its base allocation.

Thus, in theory, male animals can be harvested to the limit of the local ceiling and even beyond, with such an 'overharvest' of males, accompanied by a decrease (under harvest) in the take of females, potentially resulting in an increase in a community's base annual allocation. This, in fact, was the experience of Salliq following the 2000-2001 polar bear season. In that hunt year, the Salliq quota was 39 animals, divided between 26 males and 13 females. However, while the quota was reached, the harvest broke down into 31 males and just 8 females. The following year, 2001-2002, Salliq hunters saw the community quota raised by one male to 40 animals, allowing a take of 27 males bears and 13 females, the underlying assumption by the Department of Sustainable Development was that the Southampton Island area, encompassing northern Hudson Bay, Roes Welcome Sound and southern Foxe Basin, held a surfeit of male polar bears.

This shift to determining annual quotas based on the male:female ratio in the harvest of the preceding hunting season had implications for Inuit hunters beyond the possible change in the number of polar bears they might be permitted to hunt. It brought to the fore the role of traditional ecological knowledge as a component of successful hunting. The TEK that Inuit had always used to track, locate, and kill polar bear now possessed added value. That knowledge and skill remained essential. But, unlike before, the shift to a gender-based flexible quota meant that the ability to identify the sex of a bear before killing it became as important to the individual hunter and her or his community as the fact that a hunt was successful.

In no small way, the flexible quota system now in place requires hunters to use ecological information that was once almost esoteric to their objective, i.e., killing a polar bear. Even under the fixed quota system that functioned from 1968 to the 1990s, adult, single (i.e., without cubs) females were legal targets. Put another way, what was once akin to natural history now has ecological utility. Moreover, whereas polar bear harvesting under the previous system, except in instances of deliberate illegal kills, was an individual activity, in the present approach what an individual hunter does has implications for the entire community.

TEK and the Sport-Hunt

As has already been pointed out, TEK (i.e., Inuit knowledge) about polar bears, of the sea-ice environment, and even of the dogteam technology that the visitor-hunter must use in Nunavut, is an essential component of the sport-hunt. But, even if it were not the case that the place, species and so forth were alien to non-Inuit, there is also the fact that the *Agreement of the Conservation of Polar Bears* (ACPB) mandates that polar bear can only be hunted by non-Inuit accompanied by Inuit. For all these reasons, TEK is made an integral part of the polar bear sport-hunt.

It is clear that this 'formula' works. To this end, data on polar bear sport-hunting from 1993-1994 to 1999-2000 in Lancaster Sound and the Southern Beaufort Sea—two population areas that have hosted visitor-hunters for at least twenty years (refer to Table 4)—show that the rate of success in each was 90 percent and 66 percent, respectively. Given that these areas have experienced the combined pressure of sport and subsistence hunting since the 1970s (the Southern Beaufort, in fact, more intensively because of the advent of sport-hunting earlier), and that so many visitor-hunters are still able to attain their objective, is impressive.

However, while overall success clearly indicates the importance of TEK, it must be realized that the introduction of the flexible quota approach to polar bear management makes sport-hunt success, at least from a community perspective, more than just the capture of a certain number of bears by non-Inuit. This is because the bears that are hunted by non-Inuit are allocated from (and deducted from) a hosting community's base quota. Thus, the animals that are taken through sport hunting are as important to the future base as the bears that Inuit hunt themselves, with females that are sport-hunted counting toward the present allowed ratio and possibly against the future base allocation.

So, the ability of Inuit who guide sport hunters to identify male from female bears is no less important than that of Inuit when subsistence hunting. Moreover, by emphasizing male bears, the sport-hunt both provides some latitude to the subsistence hunt as to the harvest of females, and contributes to the conservation-management goals of the flexible quota system. There is also another attribute to TEK in the sport-hunt that relates to the non-Inuit hunter's satisfaction, which, in turn, itself has two aspects.

The first is that at least some visitor-hunters associate true 'trophy size' with male animals. The depth of this association became clear in many of the project interviews conducted at the 29th Safari Club International Convention (2002) and with non-Inuit hunters interviewed in Resolute Bay and Clyde River. While there was no attempt to expand upon this theme, other research on trophy hunting (Hardin 1999) and much of the popular literature on sport hunting (*see* Jones 1999) broadly confirm that male polar bears are more typically perceived as 'trophy-size.'

The other aspect of southern hunter satisfaction is the apparent ethos that it is more 'proper' or 'sporting' to kill male, and not female, animals (*see* Ortega y Gasset 1985). Again, there was no effort to have the trophy hunters in the mail survey or that were interviewed elaborate on this association between gender and 'rightness.' However, it is worthy of note that it was spontaneously and independently raised by six interviewees and discussed at considerable length by another two in follow-up sessions with each during the SCI Convention phase of the project.

Whether male bears are sought by the sport hunters who come to Nunavut because of their psychological or philosophical meaning or not, the gender of the bear that is killed appears to be of more than modest importance to many visitor-hunters. It therefore must be of some interest to Inuit, as polar bear sport-hunting, if it is to be a sustainable business for individuals and communities, must be able to attract clientele and satisfy their hunting needs.

For all of these reasons, the more complete the ecological knowledge Inuit bring to the sport-hunt, the more the system through which Inuit and visitor-hunters use and also contribute to the conservation of polar bear can be effective. Polar bear population biology, as well as the regulatory regime, makes TEK a paramount systems resource if subsistence, sport and conservation goals are to be maintained.

With respect to the goal of visitor-hunters, the sport-hunt certainly appears to 'work,' that is, as was shown in Table 4, non-Inuit hunters generally meet with a high degree of success even in areas where polar bears have sustained decades-long hunting pressure from both Inuit and sport-hunters. That this is the case must relate in some, and very likely large, part to the detailed knowledge that Inuit possess about polar bear—knowledge that extends beyond footprint identification and tracking ability and that contributes to the significant male-bear bias in the trophy hunt data (Table 6).

It would appear that Inuit knowledge of polar bears is therefore a considerable asset to the American, Spanish or other visiting hunter, as it helps guides satisfy the tacit psychology and/or ethos of the sport-hunt expressed by Jones, other writers, and some participants of these hunts.

Furthermore, far from being esoteric or a quaint folk skill, such acuity clearly has another value. This is because such detailed TEK (as used in the sport-hunt and, presumably also in subsistence hunting) contributes positively to the requirements of the flexible quota management regime. Given the relative rarity of any serious or consistent overharvesting of female bears, there can be little doubt that Inuit TEK extends beyond the ability to find polar bears.

Table 6: Male-Female Sport Harvest Ratio in the Study Areas (Source: DSD 2001)

Population Area	SH Began	Total Catch	Males #(%)	Females #(%)	Unident #(%)
Baffin Bay	1973	101	77(76.2)	19(18.8)	5(4.9)
Lancaster Sound	1971	363	305(84.0)	47(12.9)	11(3.0)
M'Clintock Chanel	1991	42	36(85.7)	5(11.9)	1(2.3)

As these data show, even in Baffin Bay, the polar bear population area with the 'worst' trophy harvest male:female ratio in the three population zones used by guides staging hunts from the study communities, is 'better' than the flexible quota male-female target. In Lancaster Sound and M'Clintock Channel, the male portion of the harvest is even more positive, being significantly above 80 percent. Other than crediting blind luck, only the ecological and species-specific knowledge of the Inuit who work in the sport-hunt accounts for this remarkable rate of success.

There is another point to be noted with respect to the sport-hunts' bias toward male polar bear. This is that it provides a cushion to subsistence hunters *vis-à-vis* the male:female constraint built into the flexible quota system. This is important because subsistence hunters in Clyde River, Resolute Bay and Taloyoak, as is the case in almost all Nunavut communities, generally can only hold a polar bear tag for 48 hours. Needless to say, even the most accomplished Inuk hunter may not encounter a male bear during the brief window he or she holds the tag.

The TEK Data

The TEK section of the community research instrument consisted of fifteen questions. As pointed out, a majority of these concentrated on various details about polar bears, such as gender identification. The survey was always introduced, however, with several general questions, such as whether bears were more or less abundant than ten years ago and were included to prepare the way for the main discussion. There were also two false questions ("I have been told that the sex of a bear can be recognized by the shape of its ears. Have you noticed this?"), the purpose of which was to: 1) put interviewees at ease about non-Inuit knowledge about polar bears; 2) check the willingness of younger respondents to 'affirm' something possibly observed by a more experienced person. Beyond the basic question set, respondents were frequently invited to elaborate on their observations (for instance re. abundance), perhaps followed by a question such as whether this was mainly in summer or close to the community.

The survey instrument, or those parts that were appropriate, was presented to a total of 54 Inuit in the study communities. Of those approached, 47 agreed to participate in the research and so signified by signing either the Inuktitut or English version of the project letter of informed consent. The final Inuit sample population (*see* Table 7) was selected in order to as best as possible include Inuit in each community who were or had worked as guides (G), helpers (H) or in other sport-hunt roles (O), such as fur-clothing seamstresses. In addition, the survey also attempted to include other Inuit experienced in polar bear hunting, but who had not had specific involvement with sport-hunting (also O). Finally, the project tried to loosely sample across the age range of men and women experienced with polar bears and/or the sport-hunt.

Table 7: Characteristics of Sport-Hunt Workers[1]

Community	Sample Size (M-F)	Age Range	SH Workers (G-H-O)
Resolute Bay	14, 10M-4F	25-70+	5G-2H-2O
Clyde River	17, 15M-2F	29-51	5G-4H-2O
Taloyoak	16, 15M-1F	22-70+	6G-1H-1O

[1] Three persons appearing as G (guides) were also local outfitters.

In the course of the survey, data were also obtained from community members working as hotel or store managers, HTO officers or in other capacities that bring them into contact with the sport-hunt and sport-hunters. While a number of these offered their views on traditional knowledge or other elements of the survey, these observations have not been included here; rather, only data pertinent to their contact with sport-hunting, such as information on food sales or visitor-hunter hotel stays, were recorded.

Abundance — The interviews (*see* Table 8) were intended to elicit opinion from the respondents as to whether polar bears are more difficult to locate today than they were a decade ago and whether this situation pertains to males, females and/or cubs. Although each of these questions could be answered with a more-fewer-same reply, effort was made in each interview to have the respondent elaborate as to the magnitude of any perceived increase or decline.

Respondents who stated that an increase or decline had occurred were then asked whether he or she had an opinion about the cause of the change. Those noting an increase were also asked about the season and place, if any, where polar bears had become more common (Around the community?, At the floe edge?, Near such and such place?).

Table 8: Polar Bear Abundance: Sample Responses

Question: are there …than 10 years ago?	Resolute Bay (n=14)			Clyde River (n=17)			Taloyoak[1] (n=16)		
	more	fewer	same	more	fewer	same	more	fewer	same
more/fewer bears generally	2	2	9	9	3	5	3	3	10
more/fewer male bears	1	4	9	10	1	6	1	6	9
more/fewer females	6	0	8	9	0	8	13	1	2
more/fewer cubs	7	0	7	11	1	5	13	0	3

[1] *Survey was specific to M'Clintock Channel.*

In each of the study communities, a number of respondents also offered additional comments pertinent to whether polar bears are now more or less generally abundant locally than ten years ago and whether there had been any change in one or more of the three survey categories (males/females/cubs). The only community in which a majority opinion held that there has been a general increase in the number of polar bears was Clyde River. There, 53 percent, in contrast to 14% and 19% in Resolute Bay and Taloyoak, respectively, were of the opinion that polar bears were present in significantly greater numbers than a decade ago and another 29% felt that the local population was the same.

Clyde River respondents, who expressed the opinion that the bear population had increased, mainly attributed this change to either the downward adjustment that was made to the local quota in the mid-1980s and/or as being a result of the flexible quota system. However, it must be noted that Clyde River interviewees who responded that polar bears have increased also felt that there are now 'too many bears' and that bears are now a cause for anxiety during the summer and autumn in the community and at camps and cabins that are located in Clyde Inlet and Inugsuin Fiord. No one in any of the study communities specifically stated that more bears are seen in the winter, but this absence was not pursued in the interviews.

Finally, the majority view among Clyde River respondents was that this pattern of overall increase is evident in all three bear categories. As such, 59% were of the opinion that male bears are more abundant, while 53% feel that there has been an increase in the number of females and 65% said that there are many more cubs today than there were ten years ago.

Clyde River is in sharp contrast to both Resolute Bay and Taloyoak in this regard. As Table 8 shows, in neither of the other communities was there such a perception of overall increase. Rather, in Resolute Bay, the most widely held opinion (64%) was that polar bear numbers are roughly the same as a decade ago. In fact, 28.5% of Resolute Bay interviewees felt that the number of male bears had decreased, despite the general view that females and cubs are either increasing or at the least found in the same abundance as a decade ago.

One further piece of information regarding the situation of male polar bears was elicited through follow-up questioning at Resolute Bay. Three of the four respondents who stated that there are fewer male animals today, qualified their statements by limiting this decline to 'large' males only. All three also pointed out that they attribute this decrease in the number of large males to the success of sport-hunters in their pursuit of trophy animals (i.e., 'big bears').

Responses about overall abundance among the Taloyoak respondents were roughly the same as the views expressed in Resolute Bay. Those who stated that there are fewer bears overall (3/16, 18.7%) were balanced by an equal number who felt there are more polar bears than before, with a significant majority of the opinion that the M'Clintock Channel population has remained the same. However, 37.5% (6/16) more than in either Clyde River or Resolute Bay, noted that male bears are less abundant, although two respondents qualified their answers by adding that this decrease was 'only a little.' As regards the abundance of females and cubs today *versus* a decade ago, fully 82 percent of the Taloyoak residents sampled (significantly more than those in either Resolute Bay or Clyde River), stated that M'Clintock Channel was experiencing increases in both these categories.

Of those respondents in Taloyoak who were of the opinion that bears have either declined overall or that only male animals are now fewer, two put forward opinions about possible cause. They reasoned that there are now too many hunters sharing the M'Clintock Channel polar bear population and that in recent years both subsistence and sport-hunters from other communities have extended their activities further north and east than they had in the past. To put this into geographic perspective, hunters from these communities are now encountering bears in relatively greater numbers along the southern coast of Prince of Wales Island and the western shore of Somerset Island.

Additionally, one man specifically stated that large male bears had deliberately moved across Boothia Peninsula from the M'Clintock Channel area into the Gulf of Boothia and that the Gulf was now a refugium ('a safe place') because fewer sport-hunts occur there. However, when he was asked whether this movement by large male bears to the Gulf of Boothia was because they object to being treated as trophies, he laughed.

Identifying Gender — This section of the report relates to the central TEK element in the survey: how Inuit hunters distinguish male and female polar bears. In total, ten questions, ranging from two general in their nature (Do you try to identify its [a bear's] sex before you hunt it?) to eight, including two 'false' questions, seeking increasingly specific information about identifying characteristics (shape of ears; length of hair on forelegs), were posed. It should be no surprise that while a yes-no response was possible to each question, many answers were highly qualified or nuanced. Because of this, the results of the data analysis will be presented in both tabular (Table 9) and narrative formats.

Chapter Three: *Inuit TEK and the Sport-Hunt*

Table 9: Polar Bear TEK Gender Identification: Sample Responses

Characteristic	Clyde River Guides/Helpers	Taloyoak Guides/Helpers	Resolute Bay Guides/Helpers	All Others
Overall Size	All Sometimes	All Sometimes	2No, 4Sometimes	1Yes, 2No, 21Sometimes
Track Size	4Yes, 5Sometimes	1Yes, 1No, 6Sometimes	2Yes, 4Sometimes	5Yes, 2No, 17Sometimes
Head Shape	6Yes, 3No	3Yes, 1No, 4Sometimes	4Yes, 2Sometimes	12Yes, 12Sometimes
Color	All No	All No	All No	23No, 1Sometimes
Shape of Ears	All No	All No	All No	All No
Hair Length	4Yes, 1No, 2Sometimes, 2Unknown	2Yes, 1No, 2Sometimes, 3Unknown	4Yes, 1Sometimes, 1Unknown	8Yes, 5No, 4Sometimes, 7Unknown
Outline (rear)	2Yes, 3No, 2Sometimes, 2Unknown	2Yes, 1No, 3Sometimes, 1Unknown	3Yes, 3Sometimes	12Yes, 2Sometimes, 10Unknown
Behaviour	6Yes, 3Sometimes	2Yes, 4No, 2Sometimes	4Yes, 2Sometimes	9Yes, 4No, 11Sometimes

Every male respondent in each of the study communities stated that he attempts to identify whether a bear is male or female before taking the animal. This unanimity is not surprising as it is relevant not only to the present management system, but also important if a hunter is to avoid using hunting time and fuel pursuing the 'wrong kind of bear.'

Nor is it surprising that the most general of the 'identifier' questions—those suggesting that overall size of a bear or its track are reliable indicators of gender—resulted in highly qualified affirmatives, essentially 'maybes.' The exceptions to this ambiguity were two of the youngest sample members, aged 23 and 26 respectively, both of whom admitted to limited experience hunting polar bears.

Table 9 presents the TEK information that survey participants stated was useful (or not) for identifying the gender of a polar bear ('All Others' includes Inuit and non-Inuit who responded to at least one of these questions in the course of an interview). These cues suggest that there are certain identifiers that are generally known, such as overall size and head morphology, but that are considered to be far from reliable, although of those who stated that they were reliable, a number qualified their statements by noting certain details (*see* below). It is also evident that in the case of more particularistic TEK features (such as 'length of hair'), responses were highly varied. Indeed, with regard to seemingly subjective identifiers, like hair length or shape of an animal's head, affirmatives ("Old male bears have longer fur on their forelegs than females do.") were most often received from older and/or more experienced hunters.

The significance of the hair response came out in follow-up questioning when it became evident that it was not the longer hair on forepaws and forelegs of male bears *per se* that were significant, but rather it was that the tracks left by male bears are 'brushed over' and made indistinct by this long hair. Only very experienced guides and hunters noted this 'male' characteristic.

That very few respondents felt that body size provided a reliable indication of an animal's sex is consistent in the case of Resolute Bay interviewees with their view that large male bears are now less abundant. Put another way, because of the gender bias over the last decade in the harvest and the preference among sport-hunters for 'trophy' males, large bears are now as likely to be females as males. In fact, several Clyde River and Taloyoak Inuit also noted this as different from a decade ago, but with far less certainty than was heard at Resolute Bay.

The questions about head and track sizes also drew a resounding mix of answers. However, many of those who felt that either or both were good indicators elaborated their answers by noting that, more than head size itself, it is head morphology that was significant, specifically the width of the head (males having broader heads) and shape of a bear's muzzle (blunter and thicker in males) were most useful for gender identification.

Similarly, those who stated that a polar bear's track could be used to identify an animal's sex, felt that it was the pattern of the track and footprint, rather than size itself, which was most often useful. It was explained variously that males are more 'turned-in' (as in pigeon-toed) than female bears, and that they also leave 'open' (or spread-toe) footprints. Also, several hunters noted that the track left by female bears is more 'nervous,' wandering off-line, whereas males more often follow a straight course. 'Nervousness' was also noted as being a behavioural characteristic of female bears and was explained by the fact that they either were warier of a hunter's presence or were watchful for male polar bears, while males, in contrast, were said to ignore hunters when at a distance.

The questions about colour and ear shape were deliberate ruses, asked in order to test whether a respondent was trying to 'please' by affirming a characteristic. They also brought a less serious atmosphere to sometimes very lengthy interviews.

Several questions were inserted into the survey after a conversation with a Clyde River elder, before the research actually began. These were about posterior bear body shape and the different spoor pattern left by males and females when pursued. The spoor question was belatedly introduced during the pre-test at Clyde in 2001 and then made a regular part of the survey in all three communities. The same was the case with posterior body shape.

Regarding body shape, it was widely noted that female polar bears present **n**-shaped outlines when seen from behind. Males, in contrast, reveal an inverted **v**. It was also noted that this shape was discernible at a distance from a bear, but was only useful when a bear was standing at rest.

The reference to spoor actually relates to how a bear that is moving away from the observer leaves a particular shaped trail of urine, depending on its sex. That left by females tends to be straight and roughly centered between her footprints, while that of male bears is wavy. Again, only a few of the most experienced hunters and guides made note of this characteristic.

Questions about distinctive gender-related behaviour were also asked but were more often too general in scope, at least as they were constructed, to elicit consistently useful information. For instance, at some point most of those surveyed mentioned male polar bear were more aggressive or unafraid than females, but this sort of 'observation' was often qualified by noting that females could be as aggressive as males. Thus, aside from female animals being noticeably more nervous than male bears, most of the behavioural 'characteristics' mentioned were either too often referenced to a single incident or so vague that they have been omitted here.

Chapter Three: *Inuit TEK and the Sport-Hunt*

Traditional Knowledge Summary

This section has focused on one element of a much larger catalogue of traditional knowledge, or, more properly, *Inuit Qaujimajatuqangit (IQ)*, that Inuit possess about polar bear. (For a more comprehensive view, *see* Keith *et al.* 2005). As noted, it is not intended to be exhaustive, but rather to survey a nodal element of TEK as these relate to the main objectives of this study. Equally important, while TEK is unquestionably an aspect of *IQ*, the project did not attempt to solicit the much larger and culturally nuanced compendia of information that forms the core of *Inuit Qaujimajatuqangit* (Wenzel 2004).

Perhaps the most important conclusion, aside from clearly valuable specific 'facts' about polar bears, is that possession of certain aspects of this TEK is extremely variable. In some cases, only a few individuals—typically elders who have had life-long experience with the species or, in a few cases, younger Inuit with intensive experience through hunting and listening to elders—have either observed or have otherwise learned the most subtle ways of identifying the sex of a bear. Therefore, it cannot be assumed, as is sometimes the case with 'Traditional Knowledge,' that all persons are at the same knowledge level. Yet, given the importance of the matter of gender identification to both subsistence and sport hunting, and to matters of economy and species management as these relate to both forms of hunting, the wider appreciation, verification and dissemination of this type of information may have multiple benefits.

Sometimes Hunting Can Seem Like Business

Chapter Four

COMMUNITY ORGANIZATION OF THE HUNT

An Introductory Perspective

The relationship that dominates the contemporary perception of the sport-hunt, especially when viewed from outside the North, is one that is eminently linear and disadvantageous to Inuit. As the sport hunting business is presently constructed, a small number of southern wholesalers promote particular communities in Nunavut and search out and engage a flow of generally wealthy clients (Table 10) to contracting communities where, by arrangement with these wholesalers, local (usually Inuit) outfitters expedite the required services (secure polar bear tags, hire guides, provide specialized traditional clothing) that visitor-hunters require to ensure as successful a polar bear hunt as possible. As such, it is assumed that the sport-hunt mirrors most Inuit-*Qallunaat* arrangements, with the latter providing the essential structure—and impetus—and reaping the bulk of the monetary return.

Table 10: Sport-Hunter Characteristics (Total Responses=65)

Male-Female (n=65)	Age Range (n=44)	Average Age (n=42)	Average Income (US$; n=36)	Hunt Cost Range (US$/n=38)[1]	Mean Hunt Cost (US$; n=38)[1]	Average Length of Hunt
63M-2F	37-86	57.5	360,000	14,220-55,000	24,970	9 days

[1] 27 respondents did not include their air travel costs.

This characterization is not wholly inaccurate, but it is also not the entire case. In gross terms, the direction, flow and reduction of the sport-hunt dollar is very much as below:

$Wholesaler⇒ $Local Outfitter⇒ $Guide⇒ $Hunt Helper⇒ $Sewer-'Hide Processor'

While various hard-to-estimate, and often underestimated, costs are incurred at each level—for instance, advertising and convention fees by wholesalers, purchase of hunt supplies by local outfitters, equipment depreciation experienced by guides and helpers—it remains that the greatest monetary benefits accrued for polar bear trophy hunting flows at each hunt's southern stage to the wholesaler. But it must also be appreciated, as will be discussed at length in the next chapter, that to measure the benefits associated with polar bear sport hunting for Nunavummiut strictly in dollar units can undervalue, if not completely miss, other benefits received by Inuit (as individuals and communities), from this activity.

The money these hunts provide to Inuit is ultimately invested in subsistence food production and the activity has ramifications for the larger goal of polar bear conservation by virtue of providing a disincentive to exceed the allowable catch either in overall terms and with respect to the male:female ratio (as doing either incurs economic and subsistence penalties). Thus, the sport-hunt can be thought of as encouraging the wisest use of a scarce resource (i.e., in a way that optimizes the food and monetary return from each legal bear).

The organization of the sport-hunt, as regards its socio-economic structure, relations, and outcome(s) can be construed in any number of ways. It may be simply viewed as a means to link non-Inuit wholesalers and their client sportsmen with smaller Inuit outfitter-entrepreneurs who then hire guides and other community personnel for actual hunts. Or, as seen by some Nunavummiut, it is a case of the South, through the agency of the wholesaler, economically exploiting Inuit and their resources. Then there are certain international factors affecting the hunt. Where, for instance, does the *Marine Mammal Protection Act* (MMPA) figure in the hunt: as a trade restriction?, a well-intentioned attempt by non-Inuit to protect the biological health of polar bear?, or just another example of Southerners preventing Inuit from making optimal use of a traditional resource?

All of these, except perhaps the last, represent various, but not all, Southern perspectives on the polar bear sport-hunt. And all, though simplistic in a particular way, help illustrate the nuances surrounding non-Inuit perceptions of and perspectives on polar bear sport hunting. It should not, therefore, be surprising that the sport-hunt is no less complex when viewed from within Nunavut. Just as political, ideological, and economic factors colour non-Inuit perspectives, so do they in the North, but they are made all the more subtle by the influence of Inuit culture and social realities.

Community Dynamics and *Inuit Qaujimajatuqangit*

This was certainly found to be at least partly the case in all three communities that assisted with the research. In fact, relative to other aspects of polar bear sport hunting, including its TEK component, it is the socio-economic organization of this activity that draws most heavily on the principles of *Inuit Qaujimajatuqangit* (*see* Arnakak 2000). *IQ* figures prominently in the local organization of the hunt in Taloyoak, Resolute Bay and Clyde River. At the same time, the ways each community organizes its sport-hunt are far from identical. Differences in *IQ* partially account for this, but there are also economic and political interests related to individual entrepreneurship, the internal dynamics of local organizations, and interpersonal frictions that affect the sport-hunt in each place.

The relevance of *IQ* with respect to polar bear sport hunting relates to the broad spectrum of normative action that it encompasses (Arnakak 2000). Arnakak, in fact, explains *IQ* in terms not very different from the ethnological perspective on Inuit social structure and organization (Wenzel 2004).

It is something of an anthropological dictum that, prior to its extensive penetration by non-Inuit institutions and agencies, the central organizing institution in Inuit society was kinship (*see* Damas 1963; Heinrich 1963; Burch 1975). More recent work by Wenzel (1981) and Stevenson (1997) has shown that kinship still remains primary in the construction of social relations and remains an important aspect of Canadian Inuit economic organization (Damas 1972a; Wenzel 1991, 1995, 2000; White 2000).

Briefly (and too simply), an individual's paramount social ties are to those with whom he or she shares affiliation through consanguinity or, to a lesser degree, marriage. In other words, the relationships critical for each Inuk are those that formally link he or she to family. Indeed, the core Inuit social institution traditionally, and to a large degree today, is the extended family or *ilagiit*.

As Damas (1963, 1975) points out, within this system, kin terminology serves not only to reference individuals to the system's overall structure, but also how to behaviourally relate the individual to every other person within this social framework. The importance of this last attribute of Inuit kinship is that it defines the rights and obligations between various categories of kindred. Thus, genealogy, by virtue of affirming connectivity, and terminology, by identifying position *vis-à-vis* relatives (and who is non-kin), is an essential element of *IQ*. As the data will show, this 'genealogical' aspect of *IQ* is integral to the organization of sport hunting in the two Qikiqtaaluk study communities, Clyde River and Resolute Bay.

In Taloyoak, *IQ* also figures in the organization of the polar bear sport-hunt. However, because of societal differences existing between Kitikmeot and Qikiqtaaluk Inuit, the organization of the hunt is less exclusively through the mechanism of kinship. Rather, genealogical relatedness, while important, is mediated by less restrictive principles (*see* Damas 1972b), including an individual's voluntary association, residential proximity, and availability.

Differences in the full content of *Inuit Qaujimajatuqangit* in the three communities, of intra-community frictions and the relative availability of resources and equipment needed to provision polar bear sport-hunts, together ensure that each place possesses unique characteristics that influence the way in which the hunt is organized. Therefore, each community and its approach to the polar bear sport-hunt, most notably in the social logistics of hunt organization, will be profiled before undertaking any inter-community comparisons.

Resolute Bay

Hunt History — Among the study communities, Resolute Bay has the longest history of involvement with polar bear sport hunting, extending back to 1973 when two Inuit residents sporadically guided non-Inuit who wished to hunt bears. While sport-hunting is nearly 35 years old in the community, it intensified in the mid-1980s and has grown until, in 2000, almost two-thirds of the community's polar bear allocation was made available to sport-hunters.

The majority of hunts staged out of Resolute Bay occur in April and May and are for fourteen days. Hunts may be shorter if the visitor chooses to take a bear anytime earlier and extensions beyond the 14 contract days are possible, but at a premium per diem price (CDN $1,000/day, plus re-supply expenses). Most polar bear hunts staged from the community are concentrated in three areas (Fig. 6): Barrow Strait south to Somerset Island and the mouth of Peel Sound; northwest between Bathurst and Cornwallis Islands up to Little Cornwallis Island; east along the southern coast of Devon Island and into Wellington Channel. It is not uncommon for hunts either beginning in Barrow Strait or toward Bathurst Island to shift into the other area if sufficient signs of trophy animals are not found.

Before 1998, the Resolute Hunters' and Trappers' Organization functioned as the principal outfitter for polar bear sport hunting, although a small-scale, private outfitting operation sporadically functioned in the late 1980s and the early 1990s, serving the occasional hunter-client. However, no information was available at the time of this research on the scale, hiring practices or estimate of actual success of this second operation, only that it was much smaller than the HTO operation.

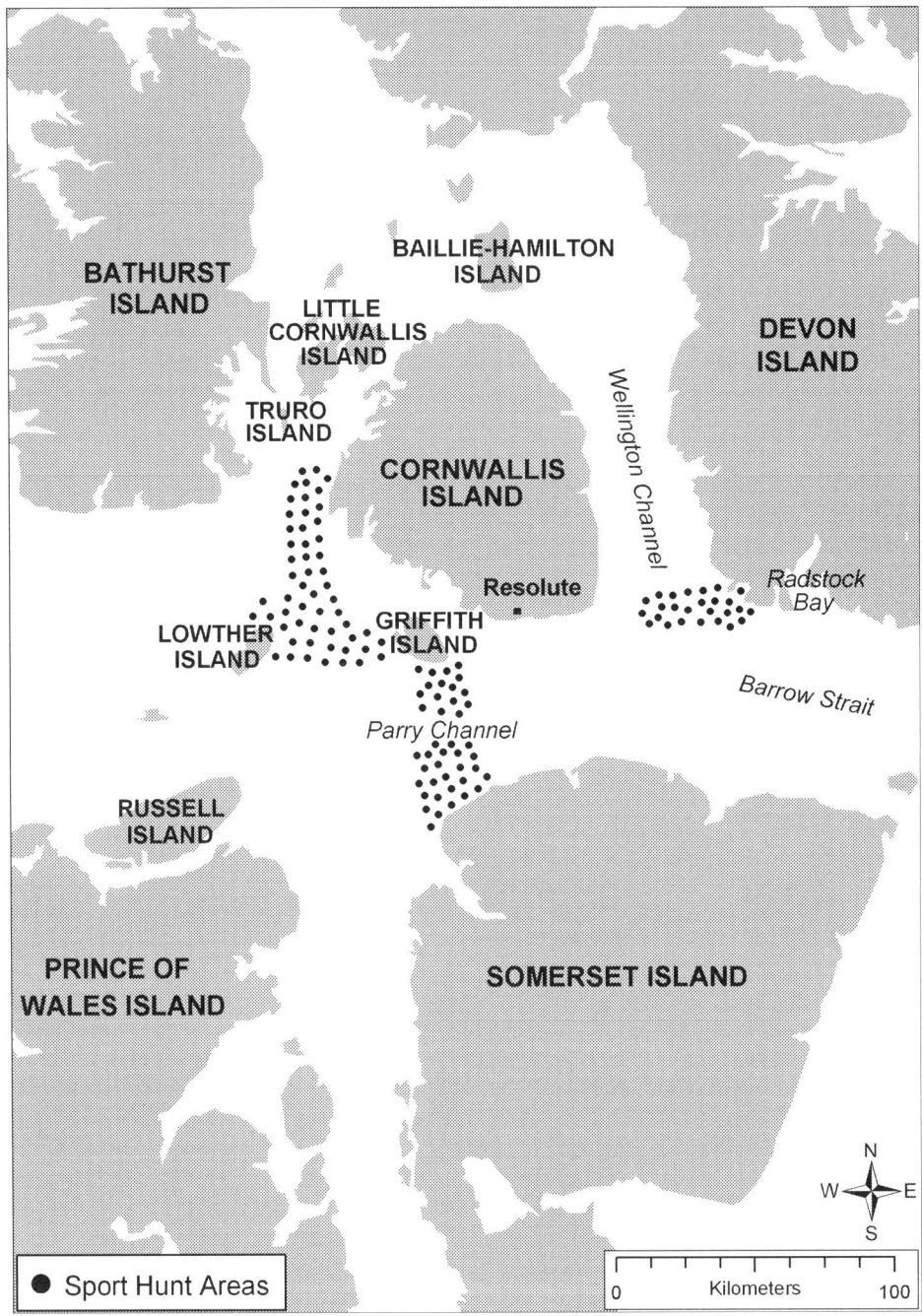

Figure 6. *Resolute–Barrow Strait sport hunt areas.*

The HTO obtained its hunt clients through a contract with Canada North Outfitting (CNO) in Ontario. The length of a basic hunt was originally ten days, but was increased in the mid- to late-1990s to fourteen hunt days. The HTO, as part of its contract with Canada North Outfitting, arranged hotel accommodations through the Resolute Bay Cooperative for visitor-hunters, expedited the hiring of guides, dogteams and supply helpers, provisioned each hunt with fuel, food and caribou clothing for clients' use, and arranged for local women to perform rough hide preparation for successful clients. For these services, the HTO received a pre-determined fee of $14,000 from Canada North Outfitting. The HTO office also maintained daily radio contact with hunt parties once CB communications became reliable, obtained any required biological samples from harvested bears as required by the *Wildlife Act* (which it also did for subsistence-hunted animals), and was the agent for the distribution within the community of meat made available from sport kills.

All the tags in the community's base allocation/quota were, and still are, distributed, whether for subsistence or sport use, through the HTO. The pre-1998 procedure was for the membership of the HTO to vote on the number of polar bear tags to be allocated for sport purposes, whereupon the remaining tags were distributed via a lottery for subsistence hunts. Canada North Outfitting provided the HTO with information about the number of clients interested in contracting a hunt from Resolute Bay before the 'sport vote' and there were years when the potential clientele outstripped the sport allocation.

In 1998, the role of the Hunters' and Trappers' Organization (HTO) in facilitating the polar bear sport-hunt underwent considerable and dramatic change. While the HTO retained overall control of tag distribution, it ceased to function as the community's sport-hunt agent. Instead, through a vote of the HTO's Executive Committee, the right to outfit all polar bear sport-hunts passed from the HTO to a private outfitting firm, Nanuk Outfitting, owned by an Inuk resident, who, himself, formerly guided HTO-organized sport-hunts.

The details of this shift are not completely clear and the minutes of HTO meetings from that time were unavailable, but the change was apparently affected by the fact that the family of Nanuk Outfitting's owner were the elected majority of the Executive Committee. The stated reason for the change was that the HTO contract with Canada North Outfitting led to the underselling of sport-hunts and that the best way to acquire full value was by changing the basic mode of outfitting operations to a private business.

Nanuk Outfitting now conducts all communications and negotiations with southern hunt wholesalers and to date has continued the relationship with Canada North Outfitting. As was the case when the HTO was responsible for organizing the sport-hunt, Canada North Outfitting informs Nanuk of the number of clients it can supply, at which time Nanuk submits a request to the HTO Executive Committee for this number of sport tags.

Nanuk Outfitting has succeeded not only in maintaining the same flow of clients at a better per price fee than was the case for the HTO, but has, since 2003, sought and has generally received 20, and as many as 25 (compared to 16-20), of the community's total annual allocation of 35 polar bears. This expansion of clients choosing to hunt from Resolute Bay has been helped by the U.S. Fish and Wildlife Service banning the importation of polar bear skins from several other polar bear population areas, notably the Baffin Bay and M'Clintock Channel zones that were popular with American hunters.

The Basics of the Resolute Sport-Hunt: Under the present system (*see* Table 11), the Resolute HTO still retains its responsibility for the allocation of polar bear tags, but, with respect to sport hunting, has no direct connection with either Canada North Outfitting or Nanuk. Rather, the HTO's members vote at the Annual General Meeting on the division of subsistence and sport tags, having been informed beforehand of Nanuk's client request. In a departure from earlier practice, both 'types' of tags are now distributed by means of a lottery among eligible residents holding a General Hunting Licence. Once the lottery distribution has occurred, Nanuk purchases the number of sport-eligible tags from individuals willing to sell theirs. In 2001, those sport-designated tags were sold to Nanuk for the set price of $2,500 per tag (price set by Nanuk).

Having obtained the requisite number of tags, Nanuk notifies Canada North Outfitting and the wholesaler begins to arrange individual bookings. At this stage, Nanuk Outfitting secures guides and other personnel, arranges hotel accommodations, and other in-community services. Nanuk's management also arranges the insurance and tax needs of the guides and helpers whom it employs, practices that were not undertaken by the HTO.

In terms of preparation for the actual hunts, Nanuk's procedure is to buy all supplies, including seal carcasses used for dog food, several days prior to the arrival of a client or clients. If possible, Nanuk has guides pre-survey likely areas for active bear signs. In the case where several hunts are to take place simultaneously, Nanuk's guides share their information and loosely assign to themselves areas that they will traverse and hunt.

Nanuk Outfitting — Nanuk is an incorporated and certified outfitter, managed by its founder, who is also co-owner with his wife. The owner also continues to guide polar bear and other (principally musk-ox) sport-hunts, sport fishing parties, and ecotourism ventures. The founder's spouse functions as the chief financial officer, company manager, and hunt coordinator. For polar bear hunts, Nanuk supplies all the needed equipment (radios, tents, stoves and heaters), with the exception of snowmobiles and *qamutik* (sleds), food and fuel. Nanuk also provides liability insurance for the protection of its clients and employees.

Since 2000, Nanuk has been the sole outfitter in Resolute Bay. During this time, it has expedited approximately 62 polar bear hunts. The standard length of a polar bear sport-hunt is 14 days, although many are shorter because of hunter success and a few extend beyond the contracted time either at the wish of the client, who pays a set extra fee for each day beyond fourteen, or weather. (At the time of the research, for instance, two guides with their clients and helpers were delayed three and four days, respectively, from returning their hunters to the community because of strong winds and blowing snow.)

During the polar bear sport-hunt season (usually March and April, but occasionally extending into May), Nanuk Outfitting employs four guides, in addition to the firm's owner, and at least an equivalent number of snowmobile driver–supply helpers (although, it is not unusual for a guide to use different helpers on consecutive hunts, depending on the helpers' other commitments). Nanuk may temporarily employ a number of women to prepare or repair skin clothing that is rented to visitor-hunters and to rough-prepare polar bear hides from successful hunts.

Chapter Four: *Community Organization of the Hunt*

Table 11: Outline of the Resolute Sport Hunt. This sequence occurs annually …

1. Nunavut Government (previously the Government of the Northwest Territories)
   Reviews previous year's polar bear harvest
   Allocate quota for current polar bear hunt to the HTO
   ⇩
2. Wholesaler (Canada North Outfitting) indicates client demand for hunts
   ⇩
3. Nanuk Outfitting requests requisite number of tags for trophy clients from the HTO
   ⇩
4. HTO Executive Committee makes recommendation on number of sport tags
   ⇩
5. HTO members vote on sport tag request at Annual General Meeting
   Members approve sport-hunt recommendation
   All polar bear tags allocated by lottery
   Nanuk Outfitting purchases number of tags required for the sport-hunt
   ⇩
6. Wholesaler markets hunts and books clients
   ⇩
7. Client hunter pays wholesaler (wholesaler or Nanuk Outfitting may purchase license, book travel and accommodations)
   ⇩
8. Nanuk Outfitting does pre-hunt preparations (1-2 weeks before arrival of clients)
   Purchase supplies (food, fuel, dog food)
   Hire guides; Hire helpers (Guides select helpers)
   Traditional clothing manufactured or repaired by sewers (optional)
   Guide undertakes pre-hunt area reconnaissance
   Client is met at Resolute airport by owner and/or guide
   ⇩
9. Hunt Begins (1-14 days)
   ⇩
10. If hunt extended, hire of additional helper/s, purchase and delivery of extra supplies
    ⇩
11. If hunt is successful, vital statistics and biological samples delivered to Government of Nunavut Wildlife Officer or HTO for delivery
    ⇩
12. Bear hide may be roughly prepared by women for shipment to taxidermist
    ⇩
13. Client departs Resolute
    ⇩
14. Polar bear meat distributed to elders and others in community by Nanuk Outfitting (formerly the HTO)

Nanuk Outfitting, as a matter of policy, provides various other services to sport-hunters. Usually the co-owners welcome clients when they arrive from the South (although occasionally one of the guides fulfils this duty), and accompany them to the airport for their return trip. Once a just-arrived client has settled in at one of Resolute Bay's two hotels, she or he is invited to Nanuk's headquarters to meet the guide and discuss weather, clothing, food and procedures for the hunt. One of Nanuk's owners or a guide also accompanies each client to a meeting with the Sustainable Development officer to obtain a non-resident's hunting licence. Generally, visitor-hunters are never unaccompanied except when at their hotel.

Visitor-Hunters — Resolute Bay, because it has a large base quota (35) of bears and allocates a considerable number (20 in 2000-2001) for sport hunting, attracts a large clientele. This is further aided by the fact that Resolute Bay, and Nanuk Outfitting's founder, have had a long relationship with Canada North Outfitting and that the sport-hunters outfitted by Nanuk consistently meet with a high degree of success. In fact, between 1993 and 2002, the rate of success of sport-hunts guided from Resolute Bay was 91%.

Another relative advantage for Nanuk and Resolute Bay is that the community's entire quota lies within the Lancaster Sound polar bear population area. This region has a large number of animals (*see* Taylor and Lee 1995) and several major denning areas, mainly along the south coast of Devon Island.

It is also important that Lancaster Sound not only has a large bear population, but also one that is scientifically known to be biologically stable. Thus, as was discussed earlier, it is one of a dwindling number of population areas from which American sport-hunters can import polar bear trophies into the United States. Areas from which polar bear imports are restricted by the MMPA can, and are, still hunted by non-American sportsmen or by Americans who do not seek to import their bear, but the latter are increasingly rare. However, as Lancaster Sound and its bears are MMPA 'legal,' it means that a very large pool of potential clients, namely American hunters interested in importing their trophies to the U.S., is available to Resolute Bay and Nanuk Outfitting.

This ability to attract sport-hunters from the United States is in stark contrast to the other two study communities, as will be discussed later in this chapter. Resolute Bay, in fact, draws almost exclusively an American clientele in contrast to Clyde River, which has not hosted an American sport-hunter since 2000 or Taloyoak, which, at the time of this research, had no sport-hunt because of a Government of Nunavut-mandated moratorium on all polar bear hunting, including subsistence harvesting, in M'Clintock Channel. Taloyoak had not, as of 2002, decided whether to offer a portion of the community's Gulf of Boothia quota for sport hunting.

Guides and Helpers — Over the last three years, Nanuk Outfitting has employed the same four guides (five, if Nanuk's owner is included) for polar bear sport-hunts, one of whom is a woman. All but one of the guides is over 40 years of age; the exception is a man in his late twenties. Each of the guides owns and maintains a dogteam of eleven to sixteen animals, as does Nanuk's founder-owner, and all have extensive experience traveling on the land, although one is a relatively recent immigrant (from West Greenland) to Resolute Bay. None of the guides held any regular wage position at the time of the research in April 2001. However, each worked a minimum of three hunts that year and multiple hunts in each of the preceding two years.

Chapter Four: *Community Organization of the Hunt*

Nanuk Outfitting is scrupulous about providing its guides with considerable advance notice of the hunters whom they will be guiding. However, if only because of the relative brevity of the sport-hunt season, preparation time for guides and helpers decreases if the Southern provider has overbooked a particular time window or if the hunt schedule is disrupted by delays caused by weather, thus leading to a crowded guiding schedule. In such instances, guides may have only a day or two after returning from one hunt before leading another.

Nanuk Outfitting generally does not seek out those who work as helpers (also known as 'supply guys' or 'ski-doo drivers') for a particular sport-hunt. Rather, the guide for a designated hunt chooses whom he or she wants to have as a hunt assistant. However, helpers are almost never taken on until Nanuk agrees to the recruitment. Unlike the case with Nanuk's guiding cadre, no women have functioned as the supply person on a sport-hunt.

The main requirements for hunt helpers is that they have a snowmachine in good repair, be willing to carry out various camp responsibilities, and be available for the duration of the hunt(s) for which they are hired. Helpers frequently work several hunts in a season and at least three who worked the Spring 2001 sport-hunt had also assisted the same guides the previous year.

Helpers work with either the guide or Nanuk's manager-hunt co-ordinator to purchase food and fuel in advance of a hunt, are responsible for loading the supply sled, and may also be asked to pre-position supplies several days' travel from Resolute before a hunt commences. During hunts, helpers carry out most domestic camp chores; if required, they hunt seals to feed the dogs, have each evening's camp ready when the guide and client, whose progress is always slower, arrive. The helper must also have traditional land skills because he is expected to spend most days traveling to the next night's campsite and so must have knowledge of the area in which the hunt is being conducted, be able to 'read' the weather, and have the skill to maintain the snowmobile away from immediate assistance.

There is also the occasional need for clothing sewers, hide preparers, and emergency helpers. As Nanuk has a store of caribou suits, mitts and boots, the only recent work for sewers has been to carry out minor repairs to existing clothing. Nor has there been recent demand for rough-hide preparation as most sport-hunters now have their raw hide sent directly to southern taxidermists.

There can be a need for emergency helpers. This usually occurs when a client decides to extend a hunt, either because of 'weather days' or because an adequate trophy animal has not been located. In these instances, perhaps two to four times a season, extra supplies of food and fuel are needed by the guide and client to continue their hunt. When this does happen, the guide radios to Nanuk's office for the support, obviating the need for the supply snowmobile helper to make a roundtrip for the material, which could add up to a two or three day delay in the hunt. Upon such a call, the manager buys the goods and hires another helper to transport the supplies to the hunt camp. It is Nanuk's usual, as well as prudent, practice to hire two extra emergency supply assistants in case there are any mechanical or weather problems on the run to the sport-hunt camp. Extra help may also be hired if the snowmachine used by the guide's helper has a breakdown and the necessary part(s) are not on hand.

Meat Sharing — Field preparation of polar bear kills is handled by the Resolute Bay guide and the butchering is done in a way very similar to the illustration appearing in Robbe (1994). However, unlike Robbe reported in his East Greenland study, there is no immediate division of meat between guide and helper at Resolute Bay. Rather, the guide takes charge of the meat until returning to the community. There, as in the ethnological literature on Eastern Arctic Inuit food sharing (Damas 1972b; Wenzel 1981), the distribution of bear meat follows a generalized pattern—and is made available to everyone who desires a portion.

The traditional pattern of subsistence-hunted polar bear meat distribution, as well as the meat of other large game like walrus or small whales, was formerly accomplished through the agency of the extended family leader, usually the eldest male member, who invited community members to his house in order to receive a share of polar bear meat.

In a sense, this is roughly how distribution is achieved in the community today. However, it is most often the male co-owner of Nanuk Outfitting who is the central figure in the distribution process. That this is the case is perhaps because the position of the firm's owner is, in a sense, that of a surrogate *ilagiit* leader.

It is also the case, as will be shown in the following section, that Nanuk Outiftting, as a business, is very much constructed through kinship. As such, the hiring of employees, notably guides, is structured as much through culturally normative social relations established through kinship as through the formalized employer-employee relationship that characterizes most non-Inuit enterprises.

IQ and the Resolute Bay Sport-Hunt — Nanuk Outfitting's sport-hunt operation is intimately connected to, and may well rely on, several principles intrinsic to *Inuit Qaujimajatuqangit*. These, as outlined by Arnakak (2000), relate to how people are to collaborate and the role each is to maintain relative to others with whom he or she may be actively engaged. These are termed *piliriqatigiingniq* and *pijitsirniq*, respectively. These concepts have their origin in the structure of the traditional extended family (*ilagiit*) and are part of a larger system of social values referred to as *tuqturarngniq*. In no small way, Nanuk Outfitting's personnel operations are not only modeled on this essential Inuit social unit, but in reality they are *tuqturarngniq*.

Nanuk Outfitting can be conceived as being a pyramid with three or four strata, in which each ascending level is superior to those below. Nanuk's co-owners, who are also husband and wife, share the top of the pyramid. The next level is that of the guides who functionally run the actual hunts. Below them, occupying the third descending level, are the supply helpers. Under ordinary circumstances, they form the base of the pyramid, although, in the past, below them would have been the 'spot' workers—skin-clothing sewers, rough-hide processors, and emergency helpers.

However, a closer look at Nanuk reveals what ostensibly appears to be a hierarchical structure that is, in fact, kin-based, connecting individuals within and across levels and, for the most part, *ilagiit*-restricted. Most closely linked through kinship to the owners are the company's principal guides. Three of the four guides are directly related by blood to one or the other co-owner: one is the brother of the male owner, the other two are brother and sister of the female owner, and the fourth regular guide is the spouse of the male owner's sister.

Kin affiliation is also evident at the lowest levels, although not to the same extent as the bonds between the pyramid's apex and the guide stratum. Two of the guides stated that they choose their nephews as their hunt assistants, with one doing so precisely to train the nephew to become a guide. A third guide has selected a brother of his female partner, while the fourth had just begun to work with a cousin several times removed from the male co-owner and the fifth, during the 2001 hunt season, did not choose an assistant who was a member of her kindred. Additionally, a younger brother of Nanuk's male founder worked with the latter when he guided at the time when outfitting was the responsibility of the Resolute Bay HTO, and then again later when Nanuk was first established.

As for sewers and hide handlers, given the loosening of kin connection between the guide and helper levels, one might assume even less kin-connection with those at the base of the pyramid as these positions are the most ephemeral. However, of the two women in the survey who had acted in one or the other of these capacities (in fact, both were sewers), one was Nanuk's female co-owner's mother, while the other sewer had a more tenuous connection, being married to a brother-in-law of Nanuk's female co-owner. Today, however, work for these women as sewers and hide preparers has become almost non-existent.

Two other relationships pertinent to sport-hunt activities and Nanuk Outfitting are worth mentioning. The first concerns a sister-in-law of Nanuk's male owner who is married to the owner's guide-brother. Before 2000 she did some sewing of caribou clothing when items, such as mittens and boots, were needed for clients. However, she is also an artisan who works in caribou antler and ivory and most recently has found a market among the sport-hunters who contract with Nanuk Outfitting; in fact, Nanuk promotes her products by prominently displaying them in the home of the co-owners, where every client is invited, and in the hotel where most visitor-hunters stay. The second relationship relates to the hotel that Nanuk encourages clients to use. This is owned by a non-Inuk who is the common-law partner of Nanuk's female guide.

This web of kinship, while, on the one hand, seemingly serving to make Nanuk Outfitting a 'closed shop' and a nepotistic one at that is, in fact, a virtual model of *Inuit Qaujimajatuqangit*. Such a strongly kinship-based form of organization in an ostensibly hierarchically structured business has a distinct situational advantage because it structurally incorporates culturally-normative patterns of behavior (*tirigusuusiit*) that already apply between the various categories of kin involved in the hunt. Thus, in no small way, the template that formally structures Inuit interpersonal relations is the template for the sport-hunt enterprise. This incorporation of the 'traditional family' paradigm alleviates the need to impose an alien and socially discordant 'boss-worker' model on a situation in which all those involved, with the exception of the visitor-hunter, see as the essence of Inuktitut ('the Inuit way').

Clyde River

General Features of the Sport-Hunt — Both subsistence and polar bear sport hunting that originate from Clyde River take place within the Baffin Bay polar bear population zone. The community's base allocation of bears at the time of this study was twenty-one animals, from which Clyde River, in the last several years, reserved ten tags for the purpose of sport hunting.

Virtually all polar bears that are harvested at Clyde River, whether by Inuit or *Qallunaat*, are taken along the coast or on the ice between roughly Cape Hunter in the northern part of the community's hunting area and central Home Bay to the south (Fig. 7). However, while both subsistence and sport hunting overlap spatially, there is generally a complete temporal separation. Almost the entirety of the subsistence allocation is taken in autumn, usually in the first three to four days of the season that, as mandated by the HTO, begins on the first of October. Sport-hunts, however, take place from March to the end of May—the end of the polar bear season as set out in the *Nunavut Wildlife Act.*

While this segregation began accidentally, it is fortuitous and advantageous to both subsistence and sport-hunters. The early start to the Inuit hunt (some communities only begin in January) means that large numbers of bears are still in relatively close proximity to the village and so the cost to hunters is reduced. Beginning the sport-hunt season in the late winter also means that sport clients can conduct their hunts when there is extensive landfast ice, better conditions for dogteams, reasonably long days and 'acceptable' weather. It also means, as the subsistence portion of Clyde River's annual quota has been filled, that non-Inuit can pursue trophies in a more 'pristine' setting, as most sport-hunts take place in areas distant from the community's main winter sealing area. In a sense, therefore, this separation of seasons has become *de facto* 'policy.'

Today, the majority of sport-hunters who come to Clyde River originate from countries other than the United States. However, through the mid-1990s Clyde River drew a large American clientele and was a much-sought destination because of a 3.4m bear that was taken there in 1993. American sportsmen come less frequently today because of an embargo by the United States on polar bear trophies from the Baffin Bay population zone precipitated by scientific uncertainty about bear harvesting by Greenlanders, who share the Baffin Bay polar bear population with Clyde River and two other Baffin Inuit communities. As the Home Rule Government in Greenland had not yet established a bear conservation management plan as late as 2002, the U.S. Fish and Wildlife Service remains concerned about the long-term health of Baffin Bay bears and has maintained the import ban under the *Marine Mammal Protection Act* on polar bears hunted from Clyde River, Qikiqtarjuak, and Pond Inlet.

Sport-Hunt Organization at Clyde River — Polar bear sport hunting at Clyde River as a regular activity began in the late 1980s and only after considerable community discussion. Its emergence was complicated by extensive changes in the local bear quota that occurred circa 1986. In that year, survey data gathered by the Northwest Territories (*see* Davis 1999; Lloyd 1986) suggested that polar bear in the Baffin Bay area were under severe stress from hunting and that Clyde River's annual allocation was higher than the population could sustain. The Territorial Government then negotiated a reduction of Clyde River's quota from 45 to 21 bears.

As Davis (1999) has noted, this reduction in the quota became a point of friction between Clyde River and the Government of the Northwest Territories and remains so today between the community and the Government of Nunavut. In fact, the change in the polar bear quota that was effected in 1986, led to the community eventually deciding in favour of a sport-hunt (Wenzel n.d., Unpublished Clyde River 1988 Fieldnotes) as a way of maximizing economic returns from the resource, despite reduced access.

Chapter Four: *Community Organization of the Hunt*

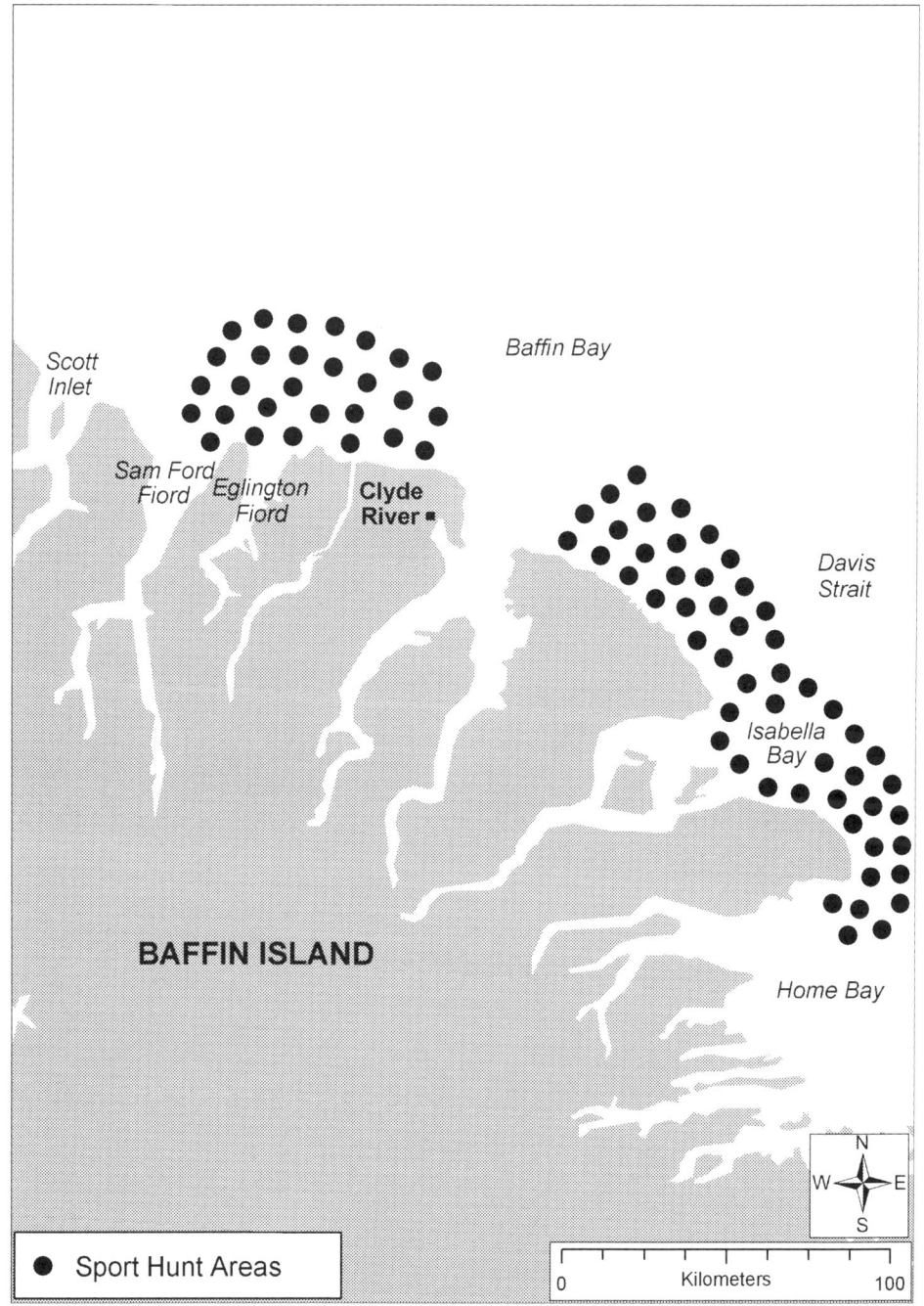

Figure 7. *Clyde River–Baffin Bay sport-hunt areas.*

Prior to the community's quota reduction and the inception of a sport-hunt, the dispersal of polar bear tags to Clyde River hunters was done on an 'as need' basis, normally after a bear had been taken. This unregulated approach to tag allocation usually prevailed until 35 to 40 bears from the overall quota of 45 had been taken. Once all but five or so bears remained on the quota, the HTO required that a hunter have a tag in hand before taking a bear. These last tags could only be held for forty-eight hours, whereupon an unused tag was returned to the HTO and given to the next applicant, the same forty-eight hour condition standing. In this manner, the HTO sought to avoid, generally successfully, any overkill at the end of the season.

The 1986 change in Clyde River's annual quota to 21 animals saw the HTO institute a lottery approach to tag dispersal. Unlike in Resolute Bay, however, the lottery was only applied to the subsistence component of the quota.

Sport-hunting arose after the new lower quota regime was negotiated and the first such hunts were organized through the Clyde River Hunters' and Trappers' Association (later, the Namautaq Hunters' and Trappers' Organization), following overtures from southern wholesalers. Eventually, the HTO chose to contract as the community outfitter (CO) with Canada North Outfitting (CNO) and this remained the North–South relationship for the bear hunt until the late 1990s. During these years, the sport-hunt grew from just three tags to the present ten (out of an annual quota of 21 bears). It may, in fact have grown more quickly were it not for the concerns raised by some Inuit over what the mid-1980s quota change sparked about local subsistence. Thus, virtually each year the HTO's Annual General Meeting has seen some subsistence *versus* sport-hunt discussion before the members vote to allocate tags for sport hunting.

As mentioned above, in its early days, Clyde River allocated only three tags, or roughly 15% of its annual quota, to sport-hunters, with these hunts outfitted by the HTO. However, by the 1990-1991 polar bear season and continuing until 1996, the number of tags set aside for visitor-hunters grew to five and then, in the late 1990s, to seven. In 2000-2001, the sport allocation reached an all-time high of ten tags (47%) of the 21 available to the community that year.

Until about 1995, the Clyde River's HTO, along with its responsibility for allocating the community's subsistence and sport tag distribution, also functioned as the community's sole polar bear sport hunt outfitter. As such, the HTO Executive Committee, but usually the HTO's secretary, took responsibility for the entirety of local arrangements for visitor-hunters, from their pick-up at the airport, to the purchase of supplies and hiring of guides, to ensuring that the sport-hunters' trophies were properly boxed and shipped South. Unfortunately, as best as can be reconstructed for at least the earlier years of sport hunting at Clyde River, matters regarding the hosting of non-Inuit hunters did not always go smoothly, but the HTO persisted in its outfitter role, maintaining a contract arrangement with Canada North Outfitting, the same wholesaler that serviced Resolute Bay.

The situation changed when Qullikkut Guides Limited, owned by a local couple, sought to expand beyond ecotourism, a limited market at Clyde River, and the male spouse became certified to outfit as well as guide polar bear hunts. Qullikkut's male co-owner had a history of guiding visitor-hunters during the time that the HTO acted as the local outfitter, but initially lacked contacts with southern wholesalers.

Having obtained outfitter certification in 1995, Qullikkut Guides Limited approached the HTO in order to obtain at least several polar bear tags, arguing that the Namautaq HTO had not managed its sport-hunt responsibilities very effectively, citing sportsmen left waiting at the community airstrip and delays in trophy hides being shipped to taxidermists. The result was that the HTO's members, in a vote taken at the 1995 Annual General Meeting, decided to provide Qullikkut with two tags for sport-hunters, but retained three sport tags and outfitted for those hunters.

Thus, while the HTO still retained overall control of polar bear hunting at Clyde River, the organization ceded a part of its outfitting operation to Qullikkut in the mid-1990s. By 1999, the Clyde River's HTO ceased to have any direct involvement in sport-hunt outfitting, by this time Qullikkut having established its own relationship with Canada North Outfitting, which also maintained its service relationship with the HTO.

On the other hand, the Namautaq HTO retained decision-making over to whom polar bear tags were allocated and could influence the overall business success of Qullikkut or any other private outfitter. This power will be more expansively discussed in Chapter Six.

The outfitting situation became much more complicated when, for the Spring 2000 polar bear hunt, a second community outfitter, Clyde River Trophy Hunts (CRTH), applied to the HTO for five sport tags, but received only two. To add to the developing strain, Clyde River Trophy Hunts negotiated a larger fee from an American hunt expediter, Trophy Connection, than either Qullikkut or the Namautaq HTO had with Canada North Outfitting. This expanded local outfitter situation brought increased pressure on the HTO from both businesses for fair, and larger, shares of the sport-hunt.

In seven years, Clyde River went from staging five hunts, all of which were outfitted by the Namautaq HTO, to sharing ten tags with Qullikkut (three tags) and Clyde River Trophy Hunts (two tags), while retaining five for itself. In 2000-2001, the HTO's members voted to stabilize the sport allocation at ten tags, with Namautaq HTO withdrawing from outfitting, and the sport tags subsequently divided between CRTH (5), Qullikkut (3), and a third, new outfitter, Abraham Tigulliraq, who received two tags. This new outfitter established a relationship with a third wholesaler—this one based in Montréal. Outfitting at Clyde River has evolved into an important business, especially given the paucity of other business opportunities, and one that has become very complex as the number of local outfitters has grown.

Clyde River's Outfitters

Namautaq HTO: As noted, the Hunters' and Trappers' Organization no longer actively engaged in outfitting as at 2002. However, its pioneering role in outfitting, as well as its continuing role in deciding the distribution of the annual quota between subsistence and sport hunting, mandates that the manner in which it organized the sport-hunt when it did outfit should be reviewed. Further, with regard to the contemporary sport-hunt, the HTO's function of deciding which local outfitter should receive what number of sport-designated tags means that the organization is at least as important as when it was the sole sport-hunt operator.

Namautaq HTO operated in conjunction with Canada North Outfitting from circa 1988 until 2000. However, while operating as an outfitter for much of this time, the HTO made no special efforts in terms of management or training to treat the sport-hunt in any way different from its other functions. Essentially, Namautaq's secretary handled most of the day-to-day matters related to the hunt and the Executive Committee concerned itself with the formal aspects of the HTO's letter of agreement with CNO.

The basic mode of operation was such that when the hunt season arrived, the secretary was hired (subject to Executive Committee approval), and the requisite guides and helpers needed to accommodate that season's client list. The Secretary also dispersed the necessary funds to guides for each trip's supplies and fuel. It seems guides and helpers were recruited *ad hoc*, the criteria being availability and ownership of, or at least the ability to operate, a dogteam. Teams were sometimes borrowed from an owner by a guide for an upcoming hunt, while both the guide and helper were expected to supply such equipment as tents and stoves. The HTO supplied CB radios when these became a standard safety item for hunters on the land in the 1990s. When the occasion arose for the preparation of a polar bear hide or for caribou skin clothing to be manufactured, the secretary usually left it to the guide to recruit his spouse or another female relative for these activities.

Qullikkut Guides Ltd. (QGL): Qullikkut Guides Limited was the first privately Inuit-owned outfitter in the community. The owner's wife serves as the company's manager and hunt coordinator.

At its start-up as a sport-hunt outfitter, Qullikkut was oddly dependent on and in competition with Namautaq HTO. By 1999, however, QGL began to advertise as a hunt outfitter and ended its ties with the former wholesaler into Clyde River, Canada North Outfitters (CNO), as it had with its ecotourism business some years earlier. For the 2001 hunt season, it used two hunt providers, Montréal-based Joe Verni and Fred Webb of Maple Ridge, British Columbia, to obtain its clientele. This change away from Clyde River's traditional association with CNO not only diversified Qullikkut's sources of clients, but also increased per-hunt revenues.

Qullikkut, unlike the HTO when it was the community outfitter, insures the guides and helpers it hires. It also has a store of equipment (tents, heaters, stoves, CB radios) to be used during hunts and its clients have the option of boarding at the owner's home or at Clyde River's hotel.

Clyde River Trophy Hunts (CRTH): This outfitter is owned and operated by two brothers and their oldest stepbrother. It began outfitting sport-hunts in the 1999-2000 polar bear season. The siblings cooperate as partners, but the stepbrother, who received management training with Federated Co-operatives, is essentially the chief financial officer, accountant, and operations manager of CRTH. He also heads an ecotourism company that functions separately from the sport hunting operation. Additionally, a second, younger stepbrother (a full brother to the manager) and the father of CRTH's three principals each have a share in the company's sport hunting operation.

CRTH's entry into outfitting polar bear hunts had a radicalizing effect on the business aspect of sport hunting at Clyde River. Perhaps the most important reason for this was the manager's own experience with the Pond Inlet Co-Operative and his contacts with communities, especially Grise Fiord, that hosted successful sport-hunt operations. The knowledge about wholesalers and service delivery that he obtained from these contacts, combined with his managerial experience at Pond Inlet, enabled CRTH to look beyond the arrangement that Namautaq and Qullikkut had developed with CNO. Rather, CRTH chose to contract for hunt clients with an American wholesaler, Wes Vining from Wyoming, although by 2001 it reduced its reliance on Vining and opened contacts with Montréal-based Joe Verni. Thus, CRTH, while still dependent on the HTO for the allocation of sport tags, is the least reliant on any of the pre-existing relationships that developed between the community and wholesalers.

Furthermore, because of Vining's interest in expediting hunts at Clyde River, CRTH was able to obtain a better fee arrangement, one that was nearly one-third larger per hunt than had been negotiated by the HTO or Qullikkut through their respective wholesalers. In turn, CRTH offered guides and helpers more generous remuneration than other local operators.

Finally, CRTH, when it met resistance from the HTO Executive, argued publicly and persuasively to Namautaq's members that it offered an alternate model of how sport hunting could economically benefit the community. For all these reasons, it negotiated for a larger allocation of sport tags from the HTO, arguing that only by being able to accept more clients could it compete effectively with Clyde River's established outfitter, Qullikkut, and, because of its already proven success in negotiating larger fees from its wholesaler, bring increased benefits to the community.

A&M Tigulliraq (A&MT): At the conclusion of the 2000-2001 polar bear season, Clyde River's HTO ceased to carry out any sport-hunt related outfitting. However, this did not lead to a leveling of the sport-hunt field for CRTH and Qullikkut, whereby each could receive an equal number (five) of sport tags. Rather, the HTO's withdrawal from outfitting was seen as an opportunity by another Clyde River resident. As a result, in autumn 2001, a third private outfitter, owned by Abraham and Martha Tigulliraq, began operations from Clyde River.

Unlike the start-up of CRTH or Qullikkut, A&MT appears to have begun in a more *ad hoc* fashion. In their first year, having received the smallest sport tag allocation from the HTO, the Tigulliraqs were limited to outfitting two hunts. Both the clients they received came through an arrangement with Joe Verni in Montréal, who also provided clients to Qullikkut that year. The connection to Verni came at the recommendation of the operators of Qullikkut, for whom Abraham Tigulliraq had guided since it began outfitting sport-hunts.

In 2002, A&MT was a distinctly family operation. Both of the hunts that it expedited were guided by Abraham, a highly respected and experienced middle-aged subsistence hunter. Because he was already well-equipped, his operational overhead was negligible as almost all the gear used for these two hunts came from his own large stock of equipment. One of his sons and a nephew of his wife, who was the company bookkeeper, assisted on the hunts, while caribou skin clothing for clients' use was prepared by two of Abraham's sisters. Abraham had an active dogteam, which he drove on these hunts, while his helpers used his snowmachine, sleds, and tents.

An Overview of Outfitting — Clyde River differs significantly from Resolute Bay in terms of both the local history of sport hunting and the manner in which outfitting has developed. In Resolute Bay, a relatively smooth transfer of the sport-hunt from the HTO to Nanuq Outfitting took place in part because the same people who are now Nanuq were providing most of the hunt expertise for the HTO. At Clyde River, the hunt originated with the Namautaq HTO, which did not manage the activity very efficiently, and then went from a less than well-organized community organization to, in 2001, three competing private outfitters. In fact, competition between operators has been the hallmark of Clyde River sport hunting at least since the early 1990s when Qullikkut

Guides Limited was created as a private concern, while the HTO remained active in outfitting, albeit at a reduced level.

However, the most stark difference between the sport-hunt environment in Clyde River and that of Resolute Bay is that neither Qullikkut Guides Limited nor more recent private outfitters have had the kind of privileged arrangement with the HTO regarding a secure number of tags as does Nanuq Outfitting. As a result, each must vie with the other and in a sense with the Namautaq HTO through its Executive Committee, in order to obtain a share of the coming season's tags. As a result, each private outfitter is far from secure and this, in turn, affects their relationships with the various southern wholesalers.

Clyde River's Hunt Clients — Over the years, Clyde River's sport-hunt clientele has been highly varied. This was due, in part, because of the worldwide contacts of the community's southern provider, Canada North Outfitting, and because Clyde River had developed a reputation as a place where large trophies were to be found.

Until the mid- to late- 1990s, the majority of sport-hunters who came to Clyde River seeking polar bear were from the United States. However, the U.S. ceased to be the community's main client source when the United States Fish and Wildlife Service (USF&WS) in 1994 invoked the *Marine Mammal Protection Act* (MMPA) to ban hides from the Baffin Bay population region entering the U.S. This was principally due to the lack of a Greenlandic management plan and reliable harvest data for the Baffin Bay polar bear population. As a result of MMPA concerns, at least two Americans who hunted at Clyde River in April 1995 (Wenzel 1995, Clyde Field Notes) are still petitioning the USF&W to permit entry of the trophies they harvested that year.

However, unlike Taloyoak's experience with sport hunting in the M'Clintock Channel—a bear population to which the Government of Nunavut (GN) closed all hunting—Clyde River was able to maintain a sport-hunt of Baffin Bay bears because there was no GN moratorium that applied to that population stock. Rather, wholesalers continued to advertise Clyde River, but increasingly directed these efforts toward non-American clients. In fact, as early as the late 1980s, Clyde River had begun to draw non-American hunters. These were a distinct minority of the community's total hunt clientele until the U.S. import ban was instituted, but Canada North Outfitters had already developed a limited client base in Western Europe, and several Inuit fondly recall guiding two Mexican hunters who came to Clyde River twice in the early 1990s.

However, by the end of the last century, Clyde River no longer drew Americans seeking polar bear trophies, and in the March-May 2001 season, Clyde River had its full complement (ten) of hunt bookings filled by a truly international set of clients. In 2000 and 2001, Finns, Spaniards, Norwegians, Israelis, Germans, Japanese and Argentineans hunted polar bears from Clyde River. That the community and its outfitters have been able to retain a flow of clients speaks as much about the web of international contacts that providers like CNO, Trophy Connection, and Verni possess (and which, at present, no Clyde River outfitter possesses) as it does to Clyde River as a place from where large bears may be hunted.

The Guides and Helpers — The guide and helper situation in 2001 was much more mixed than was described for Resolute Bay. One important, if somewhat indirect, difference is the size of these communities. Resolute Bay is considerably smaller, less than 150 Inuit, but with similar infrastructure-servicing needs as larger communities. As a result, a much higher percentage of Resolute Bay adults are wage-employed than is the case in Clyde River. Income support data show that only about 25% of Resolute Bay's population received income supplements at the time, compared with over 65% of Clyde River residents (Government of Nunavut 2004). While the main sources of employment in both communities is with the territorial and municipal governments, in Clyde River, the availability of wage-employment (and therefore access to earned income), is considerably less than what is needed to accommodate working-age residents.

There are other variables more particular to Clyde River. Two factors of utmost significance during the research were that there were three outfitting concerns operating in the community, and the availability of dogteams during the sport hunt season.

As noted above, Clyde River Trophy Hunts is very much a family concern. Primary guiding responsibilities lie with the two oldest partners, one of whom owns a dogteam while the second brother is skilled in the use of dogs, having maintained a team until 1999. The third principal member, the oldest stepbrother of these men, is also able to guide, as is a second stepbrother. Both younger men have started dogteams, but in 2001 these were not yet trained well enough for use in polar bear hunting. The latter two also have less experience with dogs and the sea-ice environment beyond the immediate area around the community, and so guide only when their older half-siblings are unavailable. Clyde River Trophy Hunts also avails itself of the traditional expertise of a cousin of the manager, who before the creation of CRTH had worked for both Qullikkut Guides Limited and the Namautuq HTO, developing an excellent reputation as a guide and dog driver over the years.

Who guides and who works as the snowmobile assistant in the course of a season for CRTH is determined by individuals' availability. During the 2001 hunt, the two oldest brothers separately guided visitor-hunters on two occasions each, while the youngest half-brother guided one hunt. The latter also assisted on two of the hunts guided by his brothers, while the half-brother/owner assisted twice and the fifth hunt employed the oldest brother's son as the helper. Finally, the spouses of two of the oldest CRTH partners do the occasional work of repairing or manufacturing any traditional clothes that may be needed and both take pride in their abilities to handle polar bear hides without damaging them.

Qullikkut Guides Limited, on the other hand, because both of the owner's brothers, though respected hunters, are unavailable for guiding work (one being ill and the other was living in Iqaluit at the time), by necessity must operate very differently from CRTH (and A&M Tigulliraq). In 2001, the owner, himself, guided the three hunts that were allocated to Qullikkut. However, in previous years, when the company had more tags, it hired at least five non-relatives as guides, including the two oldest partner-guides now working exclusively with Clyde River Trophy Hunting and Abraham Tigulliraq (a competitor in 2002). Qullikkut's owner operates his own dogteam and those hired to guide in other years provided their own teams for the hunts.

In 2002, Qullikkut's hunts were twice assisted by the owner's adolescent son and once by a non-relative. In the last case, the assistant had to provide his own snowmachine and sled. In the years before 2000, however, all Qullikkut's hunts were assisted by non-relatives (often the same individuals who guided other companies' hunts). The company's co-owner/business manager does much of the minor clothing maintenance that may be required. For manufacturing or larger repair jobs, Qullikkut pays several women in the community, who are unrelated to the owners, on an 'as needed' basis, and the same approach is taken should a client request rough preparation of a polar bear hide.

A&MT, by virtue of receiving only two sport tags in its start-up year, was almost literally a household operation. Abraham Tigulliraq has long kept and used dogs and, as noted, gained extensive guiding experience working for the HTO when it outfitted hunts, and later with Qullikkut.

In terms of recruiting hunt assistants, Mr. Tigulliraq employed a son (15 years old), as well as one or the other of his many nephews, intentionally using two hunt aides "to keep each other company and to learn about polar bears." His wife handled all the required bookkeeping. The Tigulliraqs similarly were also able to draw on the services of female relatives for any clothing repair that was needed, and had several sets of caribou clothing prepared for his clients by Mr. Tiqulliraq's sister, a renowned sewer, who lived in Pond Inlet. (In 2001, the Tigulliraq family was the second largest in Clyde River, spanning four generations and having about 50 members.)

In contrast to the way Nanuq Outfitting's guides coordinate their activities around Resolute Bay, at Clyde River none of the three outfitters nor their guides have a formal arrangement for coordinating hunts in terms of information-sharing or to avoid 'crowding' any one area. There is some informal information-sharing between guides, but those who were interviewed said they principally relied on their own knowledge of where bears can be found in early spring and on reports from other hunters over the course of the season. This uncoordinated approach seems to work at least in part because there are fewer hunts overall being staged from Clyde River at any one time.

IQ and Outfitting in Clyde River —The situation at Clyde River, at least with respect to A&M Tigulliraq and CRTH, appears to be very similar to that of Nanuq Outfitting in Resolute Bay. Both Clyde River operations were very much family-based, employing mainly members of the owners' kindred, and thus various aspects and precepts of *Inuit Qaujimajatuqangit* (IQ) are important to the way each outfitter operates. In this respect, decisions are made mainly by consensus (although in the case of CRTH, the manager-partner clearly has the greater share of influence) and the labour employed is always exclusively close kin of the owner(s) and partners.

With respect to *IQ*, the outfitting undertaken to date by the Tigulliraqs has been at a small scale, and so can hardly be considered other than a household operation. Clyde River Trophy Hunting, on the other hand, was established with the explicit intent of involving a large number of the partners' extended family. To date, its operations have included eight members of the core family, two spouses of core members, and at least one more distant relative. The familial rights and obligations that Arnakak (2000) notes as being essential to *IQ* are intrinsic to the Tigulliraq operation and are certainly present in the organization of CRTH. Interestingly, however, Clyde River Trophy Hunting's chief operating officer also believes that incentives oriented toward individual workers, e.g., awarding a new snowmobile to the best guide and a smaller prize to the best hunt helper, inspire better performance. With this, CRTH deviates from either an ethnologist's etic or Arnakak's emic understandings of *IQ* and reflect the CEO's managerial training while living in Pond Inlet.

Qullikkut Guides Ltd. has, over its years of operation, been the least family-oriented of the three community outfitters. In fact, it was only family-oriented during the 2001 hunt, because the company held fewer sport tags than in earlier years, and the owner-guide relied on his son for hunt assistance. In a sense, Qullikkut has been—or was until the emergence of CRTH—Clyde River's 'equal opportunity' employer regarding the sport-hunt.

Chapter Four: *Community Organization of the Hunt*

IQ clearly affects the organizational dynamics of outfitting at Clyde River—who works with which operation has as much effect on competitors at Clyde River as does the availability of tags. Certainly, strong cases can be made that each operator exhibits various of the attributes that Arnakak (2000) associates with *Inuit Qaujimajatuqangit*. In terms of obtaining guides and other services, CRTH and A&MT are both heavily kin-biased, while QGL has generally cast a broader, more community-encompassing net, albeit perhaps more by necessity than design. Depending on one's perspective, the openness of Qullikkut and the more *ilagiit*-organized form of CRTH, respectively, exemplify different aspects of *Inuit Qaujimajatuqangit*. To make matters even more complicated, *IQ* seems to be more than a little tempered by southern-style business rivalry.

The influence of *Inuit Qaujimajatuqangit* is much more apparent when the post-hunt, specifically meat sharing, behavior of Clyde River's outfitters is examined. When Namautaq Hunters' and Trappers' Organization functioned as the sole outfitter, the general procedure was for the guides of successful sport-hunts to bring the polar bear meat to the HTO office upon a guide's arrival back in the community (the field dressing of kills was the norm just as at Resolute Bay). As soon as this was done, one of the HTO's Executive Committee members, or the HTO's secretary-manager, would announce over the community FM radio that shares of meat could be obtained from the office. This procedure, except for the use of radio to invite any who may want meat, loosely mirrors the economic practice of *paiyuktuq* distribution (Damas 1972a; Wenzel 1995) traditional at Clyde River and most other Eastern Arctic communities.

All the available meat is almost always distributed within a few hours, with share size ranging from a few kilograms to a shoulder or haunch. How large a portion an individual might take away relates to whether she or he is collecting for his or her own household, for the larger extended family, or possibly for elders and widows, although the HTO generally reserves, and even delivers, special pieces of meat to elders.

The only deviation from this method of distribution occurs when the guide might bring the meat directly to the head of his *ilagiit* (extended family). This change of protocol began with the appearance of private outfitters, but only happens when the family head is an established elder. Polar bear meat brought in by CRTH guides is so distributed. A *paiyuktuq* radio announcement remains the way of spreading the word, but listeners are directed to go to the elder's home instead of the HTO office.

Qullikkut and Tigulliraq also distribute polar bear meat. Each conducts this quintessentially Inuktitut practice, in a slightly different fashion. Qullikkut's owner, having no living family elder, has assumed this responsibility and takes some pride in ensuring that widows and elders are always provided for. Much the same ethos prevails with A&MT, although the size of the owner's extended family places a heavy demand on overall availability. Nonetheless, whatever the exact nature of how each outfitter carries out this responsibility, all recognize that polar bear remains a food that should be available to the entire community.

Taloyoak

Hunt Overview — Taloyoak first became intensively involved in polar bear sport hunting in 1992. As with Clyde River and Resolute Bay, the outfitting of guided hunts was initially undertaken by the Hunters' and Trappers' Organization. However, whereas all aspects of the sport-hunt, except the allocation of polar bear tags, at Clyde River and

Resolute Bay have been privatized, at Taloyoak, every aspect of sport hunting was under HTO control until the 2001 Government-mandated M'Clintock Channel polar bear moratorium obviated any need for outfitting.

As mentioned earlier, Taloyoak's HTO made the decision at the time the community chose to host polar bear sport-hunters to geographically isolate that hunt in the eastern M'Clintock Channel, while reserving the Gulf of Boothia for subsistence use. Further, as the M'Clintock Channel bear population was shared with the communities of Gjoa Haven and Cambridge Bay, both which also outfitted sport-hunts into that area, Taloyoak confined its sport-hunters to the eastern portion of the Channel (Fig. 8), roughly eastward from the Clarence Islands and into James Ross Strait as far north as the southeast coast of Prince of Wales Island as far as the southern side of Franklin Strait. The greatest concentration of sport-hunts, however, took place in and around Larsen Sound.

Outfitting — The Taloyoak HTO entered into an agreement for sport hunting with Adventures Northwest Ltd. (ANL) in 1992. In 1994 when HTOs were reorganized as per the *Nunavut Land Claim Agreement* (*see* Nunavut Agreement 1994), Talouoak maintained the arrangement with ANL through the community's last sport-hunt season in 2000. When the community initiated sport hunting, only two bear tags were allocated to sport-hunters; by 2000 (the M'Clintock Channel sport-hunt's last year of operation), Taloyoak was accepting ten sport-hunts. During this time, the overwhelming majority of ANL's clients coming to Taloyoak were from the United States (*see* Jones 1999 for a visiting hunter's memoir).

Unlike the situations prevailing in Resolute Bay and Clyde River today, where the HTAs no longer play a direct role in outfitting, in Taloyoak the HTA remained the sole outfitter. In this capacity, it was responsible for virtually every aspect of sport-hunt operations, negotiating the annual contract with ANL, hiring all guides and helpers, purchasing needed fuel, food and other supplies, arranging hotel accommodations and other local services, and maintaining hunt quality control (detailed in an extensive set of guidelines which, unlike in Resolute Bay and Clyde River, include penalties for guides and helpers who do not meet these standards).

The most important polar bear-hunt decisions (where to hunt and how many tags to allocate to sportsmen), were taken by the HTA membership at the organization's Annual General Meeting. The Executive Committee would then enter into negotiations with Adventures Northwest about bookings for the upcoming season. Once negotiations about the number and timing of the hunts were completed, the HTA undertook planning for the upcoming season and delegated its secretary-manager to correspond with prospective sport-hunters.

In the early years of Taloyoak's sport-hunt, the HTA's secretary-manager also took on the function of hunt. In the late 1990s, however, and continuing to the 2000 polar bear season, the position of hunt coordinator was separate from that of the HTA secretary-manager, adding one position to the HTA associated directly with the sport-hunt.

Chapter Four: *Community Organization of the Hunt*

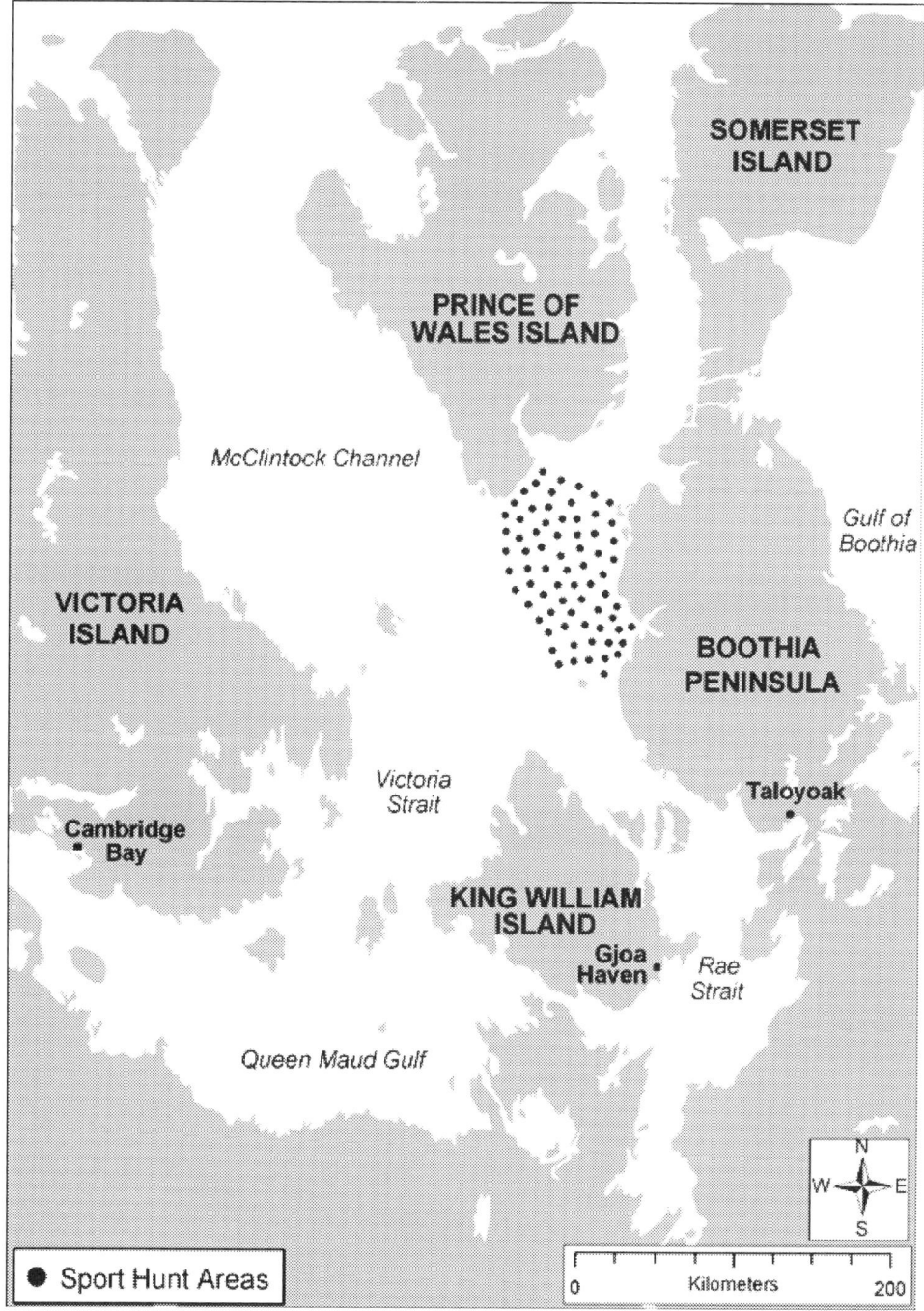

Figure 8. *Taloyoak sport-hunt areas (2000).*

The coordinator took over all the tasks directly related to putting a visiting hunt into the field, including accompanying the guide to meet each arriving sport-hunter at the airport and assisting the hunter in obtaining a non-resident big game licence from wildlife officers. The HTA secretary-manager was also required to fulfill the terms of the ANL contract, pay bills, maintain accounts associated with sport hunting, and correspond with prospective clients.

As in the other communities being studied, the hunt begins as soon as possible, usually the day following their arrival in Taloyoak. However, unlike at Clyde River and Resolute Bay, hunts staged out of Taloyoak into M'Clintock Channel begin very differently because the main area designated for sport-hunts lies a considerable distance from the community, with the intervening stretch of ice and coast considered by Inuit to have few bears.

Interviews with active and past guides shows that most hunts began with the lead guide and his dogteam departing a day or so in advance of the visitor, who then traveled by snowmobile with the helper. The usual rendezvous point when departures were staggered was an HTA-maintained cabin near Cape Alexander. As the Cape could, depending on ice conditions, be a full two-day snowmachine trip from the hamlet, it was a matter of practicality to have the dogteam and lead guide start out in advance of the sport-hunters and hunt-helper (at Taloyoak, the person who hauls supplies by snowmobile and is responsible for the camp is referred to as a 'ski-doo guide').

Alternatively, the lead guide may transport the sport-hunter and the dogs and a minimum of equipment by snowmobile to a base camp further north on the western side of Boothia Peninsula. This was done because the main polar bear hunting area used by Taloyoak guides was some three days' dogteam travel from the community. In these instances, the sport-hunter rides tandem on the snowmachine and the dogs in a sled box atop the guide's sled. The ski-doo guide then hauls the bulk of the food, fuel, sleeping bags and tents and other supplies with a second snowmobile and sled.

At the conclusion of sport-hunts, the HTA's hunt coordinator helps the client secure the needed export tag for his or her trophy and makes sure the guest is transported to the airport for the return journey south. In most other essentials, Taloyoak polar bear hunts proceed very much like those at Resolute Bay or Clyde River.

The Hunt Clients — As polar bear sport hunting was a relatively new phenomenon at Taloyoak in comparison to Resolute Bay and even Clyde River, only 40-50 sport-hunters, or roughly the equivalent of two seasons' clients at Resolute Bay, had been hosted by the Taloyoak HTA before polar bear trophies from M'Clintock Channel came under MMPA sanction. This low number relates to the fact that polar bear trophy hunting out of Taloyoak developed slowly, with only two or three clients per year. According to HTA records and guides' memories, neither altogether complete, the great majority of sport-hunters hosted by the community over the years had been from the United States.

This was certainly true for the community's last hunt season in 2000, as the sport-hunters' home addresses, as supplied by Adventures Northwest to the HTA, showed that each of that year's ten clients were American. Whether the same was the case for the hunters visiting Gjoa Haven and Cambridge Bay could not be determined.

The Lead and Ski-Doo Guides — As briefly noted above, in Taloyoak the HTO in its regulations and other references to the sport-hunt makes no guide/helper distinction, as is done at Resolute Bay and Clyde River. Instead, the dogteam guide is referred to as the lead guide and his assistant as 'the snowmobile guide,' however, all the HTA's records about the conduct of sport hunting make it absolutely clear that the dogteam guide is in charge of all aspects of a hunt. The HTA is also clear that the lead guide bears the responsibility, and penalty, if his sport-hunter is dissatisfied with either his conduct or that of the hunt assistant. The most striking difference between Taloyoak and both Resolute Bay and Clyde River is the way that lead and ski-doo guides were selected to work on sport-hunts; guide and helper selection at Taloyoak proceeded in a completely different, and ostensibly more egalitarian, fashion.

At Taloyoak, where there were eight dog teams, being a dogteam owner and expressing a desire to guide almost guaranteed guiding employment. As has already been described, Nanuq Outfitting in Resolute Bay and two of Clyde River's three outfitting concerns in 2001 relied on close kinsmen as guides, while the third Clyde River outfitter, Qullikkut Guides Limited, employed whomever was available, including (on occasion) men who borrowed dogteams in order to guide a hunt.

The procedure followed in Taloyoak was for the HTA, once its client schedule had been set with Adventures North, to post two sign-up sheets in the community Co-operative store, one for lead guides and one for helpers, at the same time announcing via the community FM radio that hiring was taking place. Both sign-up forms were posted in Innuinaqtun and English, with the number of places to be filled numbered sequentially.

The actual assigning of who was to work on what hunt and with whom as his ski-doo guide was done on a first come-first hire basis: the first name on the dogteam guiding sheet would work with the first applicant on the helper list on the first sport-hunt and so on down both lists, with the second hunt teaming the second person on each list until all who signed up on either sheet had an assignment or the number of places available were filled. In the case that there were not enough applicants on one or the other list, as happened in 2000 when only five dogteam owners signed up to lead hunts, the sequence began over. Presumably some trading of guiding slots occurred, either because of individuals' time conflicts or because of inappropriate pairings, but these changes appear to have been left to the guides and helpers to work out among themselves.

The HTA's sign-up system avoided two problems that certainly affected outfitters in Clyde River. The first was that in a season in which the available client bookings made it impossible to give each guide an equal number of hunts, the issue of favoritism, often heard in Clyde River, was obviated by the fact that in Taloyoak those who received an extra hunt did so only because they had placed their name on the sign-up list sooner rather than later.

Thus, during the 2000 sport-hunt season, when there were ten trophy hunters to be guided, each of the five dogteam guides who signed up for a hunt was able to guide twice, while the first person to sign the helper sheet (there were nine applicants in total) also worked on a second sport-hunt.

The HTA had very little need to recruit people to work in other capacities related to sport hunting because, when the community entered into hosting non-Inuit, it prepared a store of caribou clothing that was still in reasonably good condition at the time the moratorium closed down the operation. This was confirmed by the HTA's pay files which indicated that only one woman had been hired in the preceding three years to do minor clothing repairs. The HTA's last hunt coordinator also mentioned that there had been little need to employ women as sewers or to handle polar bear hides as sport-hunters were coming with the latest, and expensive, southern cold weather gear, reducing wear and tear on the HTA's stock of caribou parkas and boots (caribou mittens, however, were popular with visiting sport-hunters).

Likewise, by the time of the M'Clintock Channel polar bear moratorium, most hunters opted to travel with their polar bear hides and deliver them directly to taxidermists in Yellowknife and Edmonton. Sportsmen who hunted at Clyde River and Resolute Bay also used the services of these same firms, but, in the case of Clyde River, the air routing between the Eastern Arctic and southern Canada did not permit these hunters the luxury of traveling with their trophy; hence, it was more common to find that Clyde River women did some preliminary work on hunter's polar bear hides, mainly fleshing, than took place in Taloyoak or Resolute Bay (both communities having a direct westerly connection to Yellowknife).

Sport-hunt employment at Taloyoak, as compared to the situation in Clyde River and Resolute Bay is noteworthy in that all lead and ski-doo guides in Taloyoak were bilingual. In contrast, several Clyde River guides and one employed by Nanuq Outfitting are unilingual Inuktitut-speakers and so may bring an extra person, usually a son or nephew between twelve and fifteen years of age, to translate for the guide and visitor when they are separated from the hunt helper through the day. This youth is sometimes paid a modest wage for this service.

IQ at Taloyoak — The system used by the Taloyoak's HTO to choose guides appears to be the most egalitarian found among the studied communities. However, with respect to *Inuit Qaujimajatuqangit* as presented by Arnakak (2000), it would appear to be the most non-conformist, eschewing reliance on the extended family for recruiting guides and helpers as is essentially the norm at Clyde River and Resolute Bay.

However, as Damas (1972 a,b, 1975; *see also* Jenness 1922; Kishigami 1995) points out in his analyses of the social structure of the Nitsilik Inuit (the regional Inuit grouping predominant at Taloyoak), the construction of kinship is a mix of the social systems present among the Inuit to their immediate east and west—that is, respectively, of the Iglulik Inuit, including the people of Clyde River and Resolute Bay, and the Copper Inuit. More trenchant to the matter of '*IQ*-ness,' this hybridization influences other aspects of Nitsilik life (Damas 1969:58), including resource-sharing and the organization of work groups.

The product of this integration is a system that is less focused on close kindred and thus more inclusive of distant relatives and even non-kin. In societally specific terms, there does appear, therefore, to be an IQ-based organizational dynamic underlying this seemingly 'atypical' process (as compared to Clyde River and Resolute Bay) followed by the HTA for enlisting sport-hunt guides and helpers. This more open approach to the organization of sport hunting at Taloyoak also seems to be present in the post-hunt distribution of polar bear meat in the community. This, insofar as it occurs, seems to be the responsibility of the lead guide. However, it also appears that, unlike at Resolute Bay and Clyde River, polar bear meat is not an esteemed food and is primarily eaten by elders; the remainder of the meat recovered from sport kills, as well as from subsistence-hunted animals, is used as dog fodder.

Ethnographic Summary — Each of the study communities occupies a different position in terms of the sport-hunt. Resolute Bay has the most advantageous position, having a large quota, only one community-based outfitter and a healthy polar bear population, as estimated by the Nunavut Government and the U.S. Fish and Wildlife Service. Clyde

River is in a more restricted position, able to maintain its sport-hunt, but with a largely non-U.S. client base due to the MMPA import ban. It also has a difficult business environment, with three local outfitters competing for a viable share of a very small pool of tags. Taloyoak has invested great effort in managing the sport-hunt so as to avoid conflict with the subsistence needs of the community. Despite this, however, the U.S. Fish and Wildlife Service and the Nunavut Government's concerns over the biological sustainability of the M'Clintock Channel bear population have closed its hunt.

Each of the communities studied employ one or more methods for organizing its sport-hunt that differ significantly from those used in the other two. Kin relations predominated in Resolute Bay and with two of the three outfitters found in Clyde River. The third Clyde River outfitter followed, by necessity, a more eclectic, even *ad hoc*, approach to recruiting guides and helpers. Taloyoak presented the most egalitarian system in the organization and management of its sport-hunt, for instance in relying on individuals' initiative as a way of recruiting guides and helpers.

IQ, as distinct from any Traditional Ecological Knowledge component, appears to form an important aspect of how each community organizes its sport-hunt, whether this is through a community agency or private outfitter. However, because of the current poorly defined nature of *Inuit Qaujimajatuqangit*, the analysis and interpretation offered here is necessarily limited. What is clear is that *IQ* provides the structural dynamic that maintains polar bear as a community resource despite the privatization of the individual trophy.

Sometimes Hunting Can Seem Like Business

Chapter Five

SPORT HUNTING AND INUIT SUBSISTENCE

Introduction

The general understanding among non-Inuit, including many sport-hunters, as to why Nunavummiut are involved in the polar bear sport-hunt is that it is about economics and, more precisely, revenue. Indeed, in no small way this is how all Inuit hunting is perceived (Wenzel 1991). That money is an important motivation for Inuit to participate in the sport-hunt, whether as the seller of a tag or as a guide or outfitter, is undeniable. What is much less understood is the role that money earned through the sport-hunt plays in the larger Inuit economy.

While detailed archival information is scarce, it can be stated with some confidence that organized sport hunting of polar bears has undergone considerable change in all areas of Nunavut and the Northwest Territories since it began in the 1970s. It also can be safely said that the economics of such hunting has also changed in this nearly forty-year period.

One purpose of this study was to document the economic benefits of outfitted polar bear hunting in Taloyoak, Resolute Bay, and Clyde River and to estimate the wider impact of these revenues within each community. To this end, data on the fee paid to Southern wholesalers and the revenues that then reach Nunavut outfitters and the hunt's various workers were collected as one means of describing the sport-hunt economy. Some of these data, such as the proportion of the total sport-hunt fee retained by southern wholesalers that does not reach hosting communities, clearly suggests that polar bear sport-hunting may be less than satisfactory as a revenue-generating activity for Inuit. However, without minimizing the imbalances that exist, a fuller analysis demonstrates that the sport-hunt conveys benefits that are far-reaching at the community level.

Overview of the Data

The data of relevance to this analysis are as follows. The first is the price paid by sport-hunters to the wholesalers of sport-hunts who are principally based in southern Canada. This information was derived from hunters' statements about expenses paid before their actual arrival in the North, and almost always pertained to the package price paid by the hunter to the wholesaler with whom they contracted the hunt. Data on individual hunt fees, and other costs, were obtained via mail survey (n=64) and through direct interviews with sport-hunters (n=12). (Nunavut-based outfitters had only a general idea of the fees paid by hunters to wholesalers; their usual response was 'a lot').

More general pricing data were received from members of several wholesale firms. This information, while often different from what individual hunters reported, helped clarify discrepancies between reported costs by hunters using the same wholesaler. While most fee information received from hunters was in the CDN$22,000 to

CDN$25,000 range, there were a few anomalies in which a hunter paid a reduced price because he or she had had an unsuccessful earlier hunt.

A second set of data included the amount of money received in the communities per contracted hunt and the distribution of these funds among hunt workers. These data were collected through records held by private outfitters or from Hunters' and Trappers' Organizations. In some instances, these data were supplemented by recall interviews with local outfitters and workers.

This component of the study focused on the outfitted hunts that were staged from the research communities in 1999-2000 (n=40) and 2000-2001 (n=30)[1] as information obtained on earlier sport-hunt activity was judged to be unreliable. In total, interviews were conducted with the manager-owners of four local outfitting concerns, three in Clyde River and one in Resolute Bay, and with officers of the three community HTOs, twenty-three guides or hunt assistants, and five other persons occasionally employed in the manufacture of skin clothing or to rough-prepare hides. Interviews were also conducted with Federated Cooperative personnel in Resolute Bay and Taloyoak about hunt-related hotel employment and Co-op store sales and with the managers of private hotels in Resolute Bay, Clyde River, and Taloyoak. Finally, several artists (n=4) were informally interviewed about the revenue attracted through sales to visitor-hunters.

Through analyses of the records and the interview data collected, this report considers both the impacts of outfitted hunting in monetary terms and aggregate economic flows in the communities. It does not attempt to estimate the broader economic impact of this activity for the Territory of Nunavut as a whole.

Pattern of the Analysis

The principal concern of this analysis is the expenditures and benefits associated with the polar bear sport-hunt as these are present at each level of activity—from Southern wholesalers to local outfitters to guides and sewers. As such, analytical interest is immediately focused on (1) the direct costs incurred by the hunters themselves and (2) the indirect costs to local outfitters. At the same time, there are other direct and indirect impacts. Direct impacts are measured by the amount of the total fee paid by the visitor-hunter that actually enters the community, while indirect impacts include how hunt revenue is distributed in the community.

Similarly, the benefits derived from outfitted hunting activity can be identified as direct and indirect. Here, the former is related to net economic value as determined by the hunter and the latter reflects the economic benefits entering the overall local economic system.

Put more formally, direct impacts are those that relate to the value and costs placed upon the outfitted hunt by the customer. The economic value of the hunt is measurable through the total willingness to pay for the opportunity to engage in the activity. This value can then be further reduced to (1) the net economic value of enjoyment received by the hunter (i.e., its direct economic benefits) and (2) the actual expenditure undertaken for engagement in the hunting activity.

---

[1] No hunts were staged from Taloyoak in 2000-2001.

Therefore, direct economic benefits represent the utility received, but not paid for, by the sport-hunter. Ultimately, these represent the willingness to pay. Analysis of the costs assumed by the sport-hunter for a hunting opportunity, as well as survey results relating to visitor-hunter satisfaction with both trophy and trip, allow for an estimated approach to the direct impacts resulting from outfitted hunting. Profitability also reflects income-induced expenditure in these economically marginal communities. It is assumed that the sustained business success of local sport-hunt outfitters has an impact on the economies of these communities and, ultimately, that of the Territory.

The Sport-Hunt's Values and Flows

A) *Demand Value:* A fundamental tenet of economic theory is that participants engage in an economic transaction in order to derive utility or enjoyment and that the paid price corresponds to the expected value of the utility and enjoyment. Therefore, the price sport-hunters are prepared to pay for the utility and enjoyment derived from engaging in an outfitted polar bear hunt, or in other words, the 'willingness to pay,' represents the demand-side value of the industry. That demand exists is evident both from the willingness of individuals to pay considerable sums for the opportunity, and that sport-hunters, in response to the survey question "Why hunt polar bears," state that "only one trophy room in a thousand has a polar bear."

It is important to note, however, that the price actually paid and the price the hunter is willing to pay may be different. Thus, the true demand value of a polar bear sport-hunt may be higher than the current price, but, unless the hunt's circumstances undergo substantial change, such as the opening of new and/or more accessible areas to such hunting, this value is unlikely to decrease.

Every year, the supply of tags allocated by the local authorities to the sport-hunt—in Nunavut they are allocated by members of the HTOs—is determined as part of the total number of tags allocated to the community by the wildlife conservation authorities. This fixed supply limits the potential for the market to meet demand, resulting in a situation whereby, for any given sport-hunting season, there is excess demand. In order to manage this excess demand so that it is channelled predictably over time, it is stored using waiting lists. This helps to both keep prices high and maintains a stream of revenue, through deposits, to offset the cost of the stored value of the demand and of the networks required to link it to the end product. In other words, the outfitter relies on the wholesaler to sell the promise of a hunt before it can be delivered.

This aspect, however, does not account for how the value of the sport-hunt permeates into the community, nor to what degree it does so. But it does help set the parameters for determining the price that hunters are willing to pay. This, in turn, is a representation of the total potential monetary value from which all other value and benefits (whether monetary or not) are derived. The price at which the hunt is sold to the sport-hunt initiates the process of the distribution of economic benefits. In order for communities to take full advantage of their position in not only influencing supply but in maintaining supply below full demand capacity, they must optimize the willingness of their demand pool to pay for hunts against community subsistence use.

There is also an untapped value that can be derived by determining the difference between the hunter's willingness to pay for their expected fulfillment from the activity and the cost of the activity, as represented by the price paid by the hunter to the wholesaler. A loss of potential value occurs when the value of their willingness to pay is higher than what is actually being paid.

This demand-supply dynamic is important to the structure of the hunt. In essence, it is the supply of sport-hunts, not demand that determines the quantity of hunts per year. This represents a high degree of market control on the part of the communities. At the same time, the wholesaler, through advertising and marketing of the hunts, maintains a steady demand stream that extends over time. Communities therefore have an established pool of demand for years in advance, as do wholesalers, affording them wider margins to better weather fluctuations in supply that may result from, for instance, conservation needs or from decisions in communities to increase the proportion of tags devoted to subsistence hunting. This demand-supply dynamic has inherent value as an economic stabilizer for the industry and with respect to expected benefits accruing to its stakeholders.

B) *Price*: Pricing then becomes an important strategic element in creating a balance between demand and supply in the industry. In general, the price must be set high enough to reflect the value of the product while also maintaining a level of demand that provides long-term security for outfitters and communities. In other words, having hunts waitlisted (for a period of up to five years) empowers the local communities economically and allows them to set the pace for extracting benefit from the resource, while it also provides incentive for wholesalers to continue securing northern trophy clients. (This is no small consideration as some wholesalers, for instance Canada North Outfitters, have expanded to the point where the expediting of polar bear hunts, lucrative as they are, is now a minor element of their overall business.)

The role of the wholesaler is to not only secure clients for the current season but also to maintain demand over several years by wait-listing hunters for future hunts. Understanding that the willingness to pay may be higher than the 'going price' of other hunt activities, and why this is so, is one of the major services that southern agents offer to Nunavut communities. It is this aspect of the activity that must be understood by communities and outfitters should they seek to optimize their position as controllers of supply.

The Southern Data

A) *The Hunters*: The results received from the original hunter mail survey allow a generalized profile of polar bear sport-hunters and their patterns of hunt expenses. Briefly, ninety-seven per cent of respondents were male and the average hunter was 48 years of age, with the youngest being 32 and the oldest 86 years old. A substantial majority (>85%) were Americans. Their average annual income, as reported through the survey, was approximately US$240,000.[2]

No survey respondent reported undertaking his/her hunt independent of a southern hunt provider. However, the content of packages sometimes differed in terms of their inclusiveness and, thus, in the price paid (*see* below; also note that throughout this report the estimated conversion from US$ to CDN$ has been standardized as

---

[2] (N.B.: This profile generally reflects that of the overall sport hunter study population [n=64], excepting average income.)

US$1.00=CDN$1.50—the standard conversion rate for the time period to which the data apply).

According to survey results, the average reported expenditure on a package paid to a booking agent or hunt wholesaler was US$21,538 (CDN$32,307), with packages ranging from US$13,000 (CDN$19,500) to US$35,000 (CDN$52,500). Such a large variation in package cost is apparently due to a number of factors. First, some respondents reported having to bear the cost of their airline fares to reach their 'staging' community in Nunavut in addition to the cost of the package. The average cost for respondents whose package did not include airfare was US$17,022 (CD$25,533), while the average cost of hunt packages that did include airfare was US$26,467 (CDN$39,700). However, the former circumstance was more often the exception than the rule.

Hotel accommodations and meals in the communities account for additional discrepancies. A full thirty-eight percent of respondents reported paying their own accommodation costs in addition to the price of their agent-booked package and nineteen percent also reported that they bore the cost of food. Additionally, combination hunts, that is for at least one other species (caribou and musk-ox being the most popular) along with polar bear, while rare within the survey sample (only 8.5%), and hunts that extended beyond the contracted period at the request of the sport-hunter, also affected package costs. For instance, each extra day of hunting with Nanuq Outfitting costs CDN$1,000 plus food.

The sport-hunter, on the other hand, may choose to capitalize on such initial expenditures as airfare, equipment and specialized clothing, as well as time already incurred, by undertaking a three day caribou hunt 'add on' costing $1,500-2,000. However, only two of the three study communities (Resolute Bay and Taloyoak) sold combination hunts.

Finally, individual package profiles may differ because visitor-hunters occasionally receive special discounted prices. These most often occur as a result of cancellations that prompt late season sales by the wholesaler. Furthermore, should a hunter have an unsuccessful hunt, booking agents sometimes offer a return hunt within the same season to the same community for a negotiated and much-reduced price. It may also be the case that preferred clients of long-standing receive discounts.

The results of the survey of hunters visiting Nunavut during the six years preceding this research show that the average trip from a hunter's southern departure point for the North until her or his return to southern Canada had a duration of just over twelve days. The shortest overall trip reported through the mail survey was four days and the longest twenty-one, while the average number of pre- and post-hunt nights spent in a hosting community's hotel was seven nights.

As for time actually spent hunting, the survey data show that the average number of nights spent away from the base community was 10.8 days, with the range being two days for the shortest hunt and 21 days the longest (presumably either an extended or combination hunt). As was initially assumed, and confirmed by hunter follow-up interviews, the length of a hunt was contingent upon the time taken to locate a suitable trophy animal. Almost invariably when a suitable bear is found and killed, the hunter, with trophy hide and head returns immediately to the community, traveling with the snowmobile helper, while the guide/dogteam driver hauls the main load. Only poor weather seems to inhibit an immediate return to the host community.

A final calculation of the total cost paid by the 'typical' visitor-hunter surveyed, including additional expenses outside the package cost such as gratuities, but excluding purchases of art and souvenirs, shows an averaged expenditure of US$27,909 (CDN$41,863). This average cost includes airfares and accommodation (including transit stays in the South). By comparison, the average total expenditure for combination hunts (most usually for polar bear and musk-ox) was slightly higher at US$30,083 (CDN$45,124).

These survey data therefore provide some measure of the level of willingness to pay on the part of the hunters. As described above, average total expenditure on a typical (non-combination) hunt was approximately CDN$41,860. Nonetheless, the quantitative measurement of the enjoyment or utility derived from such expenditure is by no means definitive. However, of the hunters surveyed for this study, 99.6% of survey respondents and all sport-hunters who were interviewed stated that the cost of their hunts was justified. Furthermore, 55.3% those surveyed or interviewed stated that the cost of a polar bear hunt would have been acceptable even if their hunt had concluded without obtaining a trophy.

B) *The Wholesalers*: The study communities were involved with a limited number of hunt wholesalers generally; indeed, each originally contracted with Canada North Outfitting. Consequently, a profile of wholesaler-community interactions must be considered limited and probably incomplete. The southern wholesalers that channel hunt clients to Nunavut communities vary in size and scope. Among those involved with the study communities were: 1) a large enterprise that also operates in the worldwide sport-hunt industry; 2) a smaller, relative newcomer to the Nunavut polar bear sport-hunt; and, 3) an apparently highly entrepreneurial individual. It is likely that the size of the wholesaler, the length of its experience and reputation with a particular community and with the wider sport-hunting population, and, especially, its success in the competition to obtain local bookings, all influence the transfer of the value from the hunters.

On average, the package price paid to wholesalers for a polar bear trophy hunt into one of the study communities during the 1999-2000 and the 2000-2001 seasons was CDN$32,307. From this total, the wholesaler retained between forty per cent ($13,000) and fifty-six per cent ($18,080) for their services.

Substantial as these figures are, they should not be construed as sheer profit as wholesalers bear the cost of obtaining clients and this includes the cost of travel to and rental of space at events such as the annual Safari Club International convention and show, and at smaller regional shows, the production of promotional videos and brochures and advertising in magazines such as *Safari Times* and *Outdoor Life* and often, their own print and electronic newsletters. The exact cost to wholesalers for such activities, however, could not be ascertained as those interviewed preferred to speak only in general terms, but a modest estimate of the expense of a booth at Safari Club International's Annual Convention is at least US$1,000 and probably considerably more.

A key determinant of the amount of the total fee that is transferred from the wholesaler to the outfitter is the range of services offered in different tour packages. These amounts are negotiated by the wholesaler with the community outfitter. Some hunts are more expensive because the package includes more expensive goods, such as imported food, which must be bought and shipped by the wholesaler, and single occupant community hotel accommodations for a hunter. Also, combination hunts, which involve the purchase of two trophy licenses and tags, raise the overall package price. These latter hunts allow visitor-hunters to optimize their expenditure for airfare and equipment through the second hunt, but they complicate matters for wholesalers.

It should, therefore, be clear that the wholesaler-community outfitter dynamic reflects more than simply superior negotiating capacity on the part of the wholesaler. It also reflects the value of the service that the wholesaler arranges between the sport-hunter and the local outfitter—namely, not only providing logistical assistance, but also ensuring predictability in the market by stabilizing the demand for the hunt over an extended period. The wholesaler in no small sense creates, at some cost, a network to provide services to both hunters and communities. Not surprisingly, this effort and financial investment possesses a value that wholesalers expect to recover over time.

The Northern Data

A) *Local Outfitters*: The economic effects of trophy hunting at the Nunavut community and individual levels relate to at least three factors. The first and easily the most significant is the revenue, principally as wages, that flows to individuals involved in sport-hunt activities. A second is the level of payment for community goods and services (for example, the payment of a 'receiver's fee' to the HTO upon allocation of a sport tag). The third relates to the purchase by the hunter of local goods and services not included in the wholesale package—for example, Inuit art.

The flow of hunt money begins with the basic price that a client-hunter is charged by the hunt wholesaler. While not every client handled by a wholesaler is necessarily charged the same amount (*see* above re. package variables), data from wholesaler and hunter interviews, coupled with hunter mail survey responses, makes it possible to determine the wholesale 'average unit price' applicable for each community in the study. Averaging was relatively straightforward for both Resolute Bay and Taloyoak as each was contracted with a sole client provider (in Taloyoak with Adventures Northwest; in Resolute with Canada North Outfitting), but Clyde River was more complicated as the community outfitters received clients from three wholesalers during the 2000 season.

The basic unit price that Canada North Outfitting charged clients purchasing polar bear hunts to be staged from Resolute Bay was US$23,000 (CDN$34,500), while Adventures Northwest received a similar fee for Taloyoak-based hunts. Calculations related to hunts that were expedited to Clyde River, although complicated by the fact that the two local private outfitters and the HTO each dealt with different providers (Canada North Outfitting, Trophy Connection, J. Verni), averaged US$20,000 (CDN$30,000) per hunt. These averaged unit prices apply, as appropriate, to the twenty Resolute Bay, ten Taloyoak, and ten Clyde River hunts held in spring 2000.

The average local outfitter fee, that is the price charged by community hunt outfitters, whether private or the HTO, in Resolute Bay and Clyde River, was 55 percent and 61 percent, respectively, of the total unit price charged to hunters by the wholesalers supplying clients to these communities. The third study community, Taloyoak, fared less well, contracting with Adventures Northwest for a more modest 38% of the per unit wholesale fee. The price charged to the various wholesalers was CDN$19,000 per hunt at Resolute Bay, CDN$13,000 at Taloyoak, and CDN$18,333 (as averaged from HTO and outfitter records) at Clyde River.

From this fee, the local outfitter (whether the HTO or privately-owned), covers all costs associated with a contracted hunt (except time extensions). These costs include securing hunt-related labour, necessary equipment and supplies, and various specialty items or expertise as may be needed. For instance, in Resolute Bay the twenty hunts staged during the spring 2000 hunt season saw Nanuk Outfitting receive CDN$460,000 from its wholesaler. Nanuk then dispensed $280,000 as direct costs for guide and assistant services, $50,000 to individual polar bear tag holders, $19,000 for hunt supplies/equipment, and an estimated $1,000-2,000 for unexpected expenses. Conservatively, just over 76%, or CDN$351,000, of the total fees received from Canadian North Outfitting were expended as direct business costs. Of this amount, 94 percent went to individuals in the community.

While wages to guides and other workers involved in the sport-hunt are obvious, less so is the benefit to the community obtained through the fees local outfitters pay for their sport tags. Such tag payments occur in two of the three communities, Resolute Bay and Clyde River; in Taloyoak, as the HTO is also the outfitter, no tag fee is charged.

While the outfitters in Resolute Bay and Clyde River pay for the tags that will be used by their sport-hunt clients, there is an essential difference between the two situations. In Resolute, the local outfitter purchases tags for the non-Inuit hunt directly from members of the community; in Clyde River, sport tags are purchased from the Namautaq Hunters' and Trappers' Organization.

In Resolute, payments are made to HTO members who acquired a polar bear tag through the HTO-sponsored community lottery. In practice, no tags are actually allocated to sport-hunting. Rather, the HTO membership votes a number of tags from the overall community quota that may be sold by individual tag holders for the purpose of outfitted hunting. The local outfitting concern, Nanuk Outfitting, then purchases as many of the 'sport tags' as its clientele will require up to the ceiling that was voted by the HTO's members. In the 2000 and 2001 sport-hunt seasons, the tag price was CDN$2,500 and the 20 tags that were available from individual holders in each of those years were acquired by Nanuk Outfitting. As a result of these purchases, CDN$50,000 was received by Resolute Inuit who had no direct involvement in the sport-hunt, but no monetary benefit accrued directly to the community as a whole.

This is in contrast to the situation in Clyde River. There, HTO members vote annually to allocate the number of tags that will be set aside for sport-hunt purposes (10 in 2000), but none of these tags enter the general lottery. Rather, the private outfitters in the community, Clyde Trophy Hunts and Qullikkut in 2000 and Clyde Trophy Hunts, Qullikkut and Abraham Tigulliraq in 2001, purchase these set-asides directly from the HTO. In 1999-2000, outfitters purchased eight of the sport tags for CDN$2,000 each; two of the available 10 were bought for $2,500 each. The money the HTO receives from the outfitters ($21,000) for these tags is used to purchase ammunition, CB radios and survival suits, which the organization then makes available to community hunters at cost. In this respect, there is a certain benefit to the entire community, especially as most adult males and many adult women hold HTO membership.

B) *Guides and Helpers*: Virtually all the guides and hunt assistants who were interviewed in the course of the research derive a substantial portion of their cash income from this employment. No guide or helper who was interviewed held full-time employment at the time. However, employment histories elicited in the course of these interviews showed that all had at one time or another been involved in some type of seasonal or casual work other than guiding. This included summer employment as part-time construction workers and on-call truck drivers working for the municipality, jobs that typically paid between $18.00 and $25.00 per hour. Further, three stated that their construction employment had lasted for two consecutive months. Three of the Resolute Bay guides and two from Clyde River had also been involved in eco-tourism guiding, such as dogteam drivers on the late spring ice, or boaters transporting climbers and hikers. Only one received a substantial income from government transfers (in this case, disability) benefits.

The wage rates for sport-hunt workers differ, based on the responsibilities and expertise of individuals, guides always being remunerated at a higher rate than hunt assistants. Also, more obviously, hunt employee wages vary between communities by virtue of differences in the basic fee agreements that local outfitters have negotiated with southern wholesalers.

Generally speaking, the higher the fee arrangement between wholesaler and outfitter, the higher the wage rate for the most pivotal hunt workers—the guides and hunt assistants. At Resolute Bay, where the sole outfitter receives CDN$19,000 for services provided to each southern client, dogteam guides are paid CDN$9,000 per 10 day hunt and their assistants $5,000.

On the other hand, in Taloyoak the basic per client fee is CDN$13,000. As a result, dogteam guides there received a more modest wage of $4,300, that could increase to $4,800 as the Taloyoak-Adventures North contract included a $500 guides' bonus for each successful hunt. However, no such bonuses were available to snowmobile guides, whose wage was set at a flat $3,800 per hunt.

The modest basic per-hunt fee at Taloyoak almost certainly related to the fact that the community was relatively new to polar bear sport hunting, having only become involved circa 1992. It also became apparent during the time spent in the community that the sole local outfitter, the Hunters' and Trappers' Organization, had scant awareness of the fee arrangements existing between outfitters in other communities and their southern wholesalers. This was in marked contrast to the level of knowledge about these arrangements in Resolute Bay and Clyde River where it was found that, for example, Clyde River Trophy Hunts (CRTH) knew what level of fee was received in Pond Inlet and Grise Fiord. In fact, CRTH's manager had consulted with the Grise Fiord HTO about the best (highest paying) wholesaler with whom the latter had dealt.

Clyde River, because of multiple local outfitters using different wholesalers, presented the most complex economic situation of the three study communities. In 2001, both Qullikkut Guides Limited and A&M Tigulliraq contracted with their respective southern wholesalers to provide hunts at CDN$18,000 per client, while Clyde River Trophy Hunts, as noted above, following consultations with Grise Fiord, sold its hunts for $19,000.

Such differences also exist with respect to the wage paid to guides and helpers. Two of the Clyde River outfitters paid their dogteam guides $5,000 for each hunt worked, with one using an incentive system through which the 'best' guide and 'best' helper received a cash bonus at the end of the outfitted hunting season. The third outfitter paid his guides at the flat rate of $5,500. The pay differential between outfitters with regard to hunt helpers was even larger. One firm paid this group at a rate of $4,500 per hunt, while the other two compensated helpers at $4,000 and $2,000.

Despite the difference between the overall fee received by CRTH and the then other outfitters at Clyde River, generally the wages received by guides and helpers, except for the lowest rate paid by A&M Tigulliraq to its hunt assistant (the owner's son), were above the levels of remuneration that existed when the Clyde River's HTO expedited polar bear hunts. The reason for this is that the contract that Namautaq HTO held with its southern wholesaler underwent almost no change in the roughly ten years that it was the only outfitter in the community. The original payment received by the HTO was CDN$13,500 per hunt, rising in the late 1990s to $15,000.

There is an interesting aspect to the Clyde River HTO's arrangement with the southern wholesaler with whom it contracted during this period. The higher end figure was available only if Clyde River provided a certain number of tags from the community quota to the sport-hunt. It appears likely that the Clyde River's HTO was the only local outfitting organization whose wholesaler contract contained such a provision.

The nature of this arrangement is exemplified by the HTO's 1999 contact with Canada North Outfitting. In that year, the agreement stipulated that if no more than three sport tags were allocated, then the fee received for each tag would be $13,500. However, the agreement contained an 'escalator clause' in which the per tag fee received by Namautaq would rise to $13,750 if four sport tags were provided and $14,000 per-tag for five tags, with the progression jumping to $14,500 for six and then $15,000 for seven or more tags. (The preceding year, 1998, the progression was from $13,000 for each of the first three tags provided to $14,000 per tag for up to seven or more, presumably an indication that Namautaq was taking advantage of the community's popularity as a sport-hunt destination.)

This suggests two things. First, that the Clyde River's wholesaler at the time was amply aware of buyer demand. The other is that this low-high price per polar bear tag progression had the potential to create an essential conflict between the economic needs and the subsistence/cultural interests of the community.

C) *Other Workers*: With regard to wage data for other catagories of hunt workers, such as the women who manufactured caribou clothing for trophy hunters' use, the information available is much more limited than it was for either guides or hunt assistants. Indeed, in most cases, there were few actual records of such transactions and, thus the study had to rely upon individual recall.

At Resolute Bay, major repairs to caribou clothing were compensated at $500 per repair job. While no data were available from Clyde River on clothing repairs, one outfitter reported paying $1,500 for a complete caribou suit and another paid $1,000, while the third paid $100 per pair of caribou mittens. A similar paucity of data existed in Taloyoak, with the 2000 season data showing only that $40.00 had been paid for repairs to a pair of caribou mittens.

The same paucity of information pertained to fees paid to women for rough preparation of polar bear hides. Only the Taloyoak HTO's files held any such record, showing that in 1999 a woman was paid $350 for rough preparation. Clyde River outfitters reported a pay range for such work from a low of $300 to $500. (In 1994, the author arranged for a woman to be paid $450 to scrape and stretch a polar bear hide for a hunter). Given the labour involved in even rough fleshing of a large polar bear skin ($\approx$ 5-8 hours), this work seemed to be under-remunerated. In both Clyde River and Resolute Bay, the women employed to rough-prepare fresh hides were always relatives of either the outfitter or of the guide from that particular hunt. The same seemed to be the case with skin clothing manufacture and repair.

Another role associated with the sport-hunt is that of hunt coordinator. Among the communities studied, only the Taloyoak HTO exclusively employed a person to coordinate the purchase of hunt supplies and to greet arriving hunters (*see* Chapter 4— Community Organization of the Hunt section). During the 2000 sport-hunt, this effort was paid at the rate of $250.00 per hunt. None of the private outfitters from Resolute Bay or Clyde River employed such a person, this role being carried out by the outfitters' owner or business manager, and it seems that even when the HTOs in those communities were the outfitters, the organization's secretary-manager served as hunt coordinator.

The hunt does generate local employment benefits beyond those going to persons directly involved as guides or in other capacities. Probably the most significant benefits are gained by the local hotels. Unfortunately, data about the exact economic impact that the presence of sport-hunters has on this component of the community economy are very imprecise.

At Resolute Bay, each of the two hotels regularly employs at least one cleaning person and a cook when one or more guests are present. However, because the dining areas of both hotels are open for twice-daily coffee breaks available to government employees, it would appear that the presence of a hunter or two would have only a marginal effect. On the other hand, in Taloyoak (two hotels) and Clyde River (one hotel), these establishments would not open on any day unless they had guests staying at the hotel.

Nonetheless, it is possible to loosely, and conservatively, estimate the employment effect of hunters in Clyde River and Taloyoak, where the wages paid to cooks ($20.00 per hour) and maids ($12.00) would otherwise be foregone if the establishments were not open. If, as was reported through the project mail survey, the average local hotel stay of a sport-hunter is 7.05 days, the services of a cleaner would be required each day of the stay for at least three hours (this estimate is based on the situation in Clyde River when only one or two guests are present). There would be similar, if not slightly more working hours for the cook and it is highly probable that a kitchen helper-dishwasher might also be hired ($8.00-10.00/hour). Thus, during the period when sport-hunters are present, a cook might earn between $5,000-6,000 for the season (assuming an average stay of 7 days per hunter), while maids might earn up to $3,000 for the same period.

D) *Other Hunt Benefits*: Guides, helpers, and visitor-hunters all noted that at the conclusion of most sport-hunts, the guides and their helpers received various gratuities. These were usually in the form of cash, often in U.S. dollars. It was also a frequent occurrence for hunt clients to give equipment and clothing to their guides and, sometimes, to the snowmobile helper.

Using the detailed information available from the sport-hunter mail survey, sport-hunt clients reported that on average the principal guide received a cash tip of CDN$1,100 and assistants tips in the range of $550-600. While only 89% of the survey's respondents reported giving cash gratuities, none of the guides subsequently interviewed stated that they had not received some form of cash gratuity at the conclusion of a hunt, whether successful or not. On the other hand, helpers seemed to not always have been treated with such generosity, according to reports by several Clyde River men.

The non-cash gratuities that pass from sport-hunters to hunt guides or assistants were more difficult to quantify. This is because the item(s) received were later not always in the possession of the receiving guide or were of a manufacture that made it difficult to track the original cost. However, the following items received by Clyde River and Resolute Bay guides provide some idea of the value of items received. Among the gifts given at the end of various hunts were a Sako .375 cal. rifle (US$2,500), Zeiss binoculars (approximately US$1,000), a compound hunting bow with arrows, and a Garmin GPS locator (CDN$400-500). In addition, expensive down parkas and pants and various styles of cold weather footwear were also given to Inuit. By and large, these non-cash, but highly valued 'tips' (e.g., rifles) were given to the principal guide of a hunt, with assistants more often receiving expensive items of clothing.

Survey data also allow estimates of the average purchase of Inuit art and handicrafts by hunters during their stay. These data show that about half (55 per cent) of respondents purchased art or handicrafts having an average value of CDN $1,627 per purchaser. Whether such purchases took place, however, depended on: 1) the length of a hunter's post-trip stay, with arts and crafts more often being bought if a hunter had at least a two-day wait for his or her departing flight south; and, 2) the willingness of either the visitor to venture into the community or, conversely, the willingness of Inuit to visit the community hotel in order to offer art and crafts to potential customers (in Clyde River, for instance, the hotel owner discouraged such visitations).

It should be noted that not all visitor-hunter purchases were necessarily expensive items such as sculptures and prints. In 1994, when three trophy hunters at Clyde River were delayed by bad weather conditions, a situation in which they were reticent to venture away from the hotel, a young man showed them metal harpoon heads and ulus that had been made by an elderly man who, himself, was shy about visiting the hotel. After being shown an example of each 'artifact,' the hunters purchased the elder's entire surplus of each, 14 ulus and 11 harpoons, at $20 each, noting that the items would make handy gifts for various clients of their southern businesses.

E) *Income in Kind*: As best that can be ascertained, most sport-hunters, aside from perhaps having a meal of polar bear meat while camping, have little interest in the meat from the animals they hunt. Guides and helpers, however, appear to always ensure this meat is returned and distributed in their communities (*see* Organization of the Hunt).

While no data exist on the monetary value of polar bear meat as food, assigning an imputed value to country food (Wenzel 1997) has become relatively common as a means of estimating the replacement cost of traditional dietary items. Such a calculation is generally done by assigning a dollar per kilogram value to the edible meat obtained from a hunt, usually based on the average retail cost of a range of imported frozen meats available in the local store. An approximate substitution value is derived through the following conversions (*see* Wenzel and White 2000):

[Harvest Live Weight(kg)⇒Edible Weight(kg)⇒Equivalent Store Food(kg)⇒

Average Price of Store Food=Imputed Value of the Edible Weight]

Foote (1967:141) estimated that the average adult polar bear weighs approximately 363.6kg and that 38 percent of this weight is edible meat tissue (approx. 140kg). Using a rounded average figure of $8.50 per kilo for frozen imported meats available at Resolute Bay's Co-operative Store, the average adult bear thus yields the equivalent of CDN$1,190 (140 X $8.50) of food, or around $24,000 for the entire sport quota. Because of higher retail prices in Taloyoak and Clyde River, it is suggested that a per kilo country food 'price' of $10.00 more accurately reflects imported food costs in those communities. Thus, the equivalent value of the ten bears allocated to sport hunting at Clyde is $14,000, while the value at Taloyoak is computed as being only $1,500-2,500 as polar bear meat there is usually used as dog food (25kg bags of imported dog food cost up to $60.00 at the community store).

Chapter Five: *Sport Hunting and Inuit Subsistence*

Section Summary and Observations

Summary presentation of the economic data from the sport-hunt as it occurs in each of the research communities is complex. Inter-community, and even intra-community, comparisons are difficult because some types of information remain, at best, partial or speculative. However, the following tables provide concise overviews of the general pattern of this activity (Table 12) and the monetary and in-kind benefits and costs in Taloyoak, Clyde River and Resolute Bay (Table 13).

Table 12: Generalized Pattern of Outfitted Hunts

Steps	Activities and Timing
1	DSD review of community's previous year's harvest
2	DSD approval of upcoming year's quota (August)
3	Wholesaler informs HTO and/or private outfitter(s) of client interest
4	Allocation of tags for subsistence and sport-hunts at HTO AGM (August)
4a	HTO allocates sport tags to local outfitter(s) (Autumn)
5	HTO and/or outfitter(s) inform wholesaler of available tags (as above)
6	Community hunts marketed and sold by wholesaler (Autumn-Winter)
7	Wholesaler and local outfitter(s) contract for upcoming season's hunts (above)
8	Sport-hunter pays wholesaler, booking dates confirmed, license obtained and schedule for accommodations and transportation are received (2-3 months)
9	Community pre-hunt preparations (1 month to 1 day prior to hunt)
9a	Local expeditor purchases store supplies, hires guides
9b	Guides hire helpers
9c	Supplies pre-positioned and hunt area surveyed (optional)
9d	Sport hunter arrives, pre-hunt orientation (1 day)
10	Hunt (1-14 days)
10a	Extension (optional)
11	Return, report vital statistics if successful, and obtain export tag (1 day)
11a	Hunter departs (1-3 days), Distribution of polar bear meat within community
11b	Hide 'rough-prepared,' defleshed and shipped (5-10 days)

Several observations about these data are worthy of note. The first concerns cross-community comparison of outfitter net revenues presented in Table 13.

Despite the very different modes of hunt organization found in each of the study communities, the revenue derived at each place per sport-hunt, excluding roughly estimated items like hotel employees' wages, is remarkably close: $30,910 in Taloyoak, $33,000 in Resolute Bay and $27,430 in Clyde River. That such wide variance appears to exist between Clyde River and Resolute Bay probably relates as much to the absence of certain information from the latter community summary than to any inefficiencies at Clyde River.

A second observation is more inferential: given the present considerable cost of this type of outfitted hunt to sportsmen and the limited availability of the good being sought (*viz.* polar bears), it seems reasonable to suggest that the hunt suffers from under-valuation in the communities.

Table 13: Economic Attributes of Polar Bear Sport Hunting [1]

GENERAL ATTRIBUTES	CLYDE RIVER	RESOLUTE BAY	TALOYOAK
A) Annual Polar Bear Quota	21	35	20
B) Annual Sport-Hunts	10	20	10
C) Local Outfitters	3 (private)	1 (private)	1 (community)
D) Wholesale Hunt Price[2]	$30,000	$34,500	$34,500
E) Local Outfitter Price[3]	$18,400	$19,000	$13,000
LOCAL DISTRIBUTION			
F) Guides/Helpers	10/10	5/9	5/9
G) Total Guides' Wages	$51,000	$180,000	$47,300
H) Total Helpers' Wages	$41,000	$100,000	$38,200
I) Gratuities (average per hunt)	$1,800	$2,300	$1,500
J) Equipment Capitalization[4]	$42,000	$ 34,000	Unknown
K) Polar Bear Meat (kg)	1,400	3,000	1,400
L) PB Meat $ Value[5]	$14,000	$25,000	$2,000[6]

[1] Not factored in are fees to polar bear tag holders, additional charter or scheduled airline fares, local purchases of arts and handicrafts, and the cost of hunt consumables (food).
[2] Total fee paid to southern broker by the individual hunter for his/her hunt (CDN$).
[3] Contract fee between southern-based wholesaler and local outfitters.
[4] These data refer to equipment purchased with sport-hunt wages and are only partial.
[5] Based on $8.50 per kg of imported meat (averaged across the communities).
[6] As polar bear meat is generally used for dog fodder at Taloyoak, the value imputed to the meat entering the community is based on the price of imported dry dog food.

The experience of Resolute Bay is instructive in this regard. There, despite the cost of its outfitted hunts, Nanuk Outfitting appears to have experienced no difficulty in attracting twenty hunters each season in recent years. Undoubtedly, this is in no small way attributable to the strong marketing efforts of Canada North Outfitting and, perhaps, to the fact that some bear population in other areas of the Canadian Arctic formerly open to sport hunting are now closed, or at least restricted as to clientele. Nonetheless, both quantitative hunt data and hunter survey and interview responses make it clear that polar bear are highly desired as sport trophies. Further, in light of the limited number of bears annually available to the trophy market (about 90 in 2000-2001), polar bear sport-hunting most likely can command value above that presently received.

There is one other element to outfitted hunting that is worthy of note: the income that this activity provides to Inuit is, in a very real sense, 'new money' and is understood by local outfitters, guides, and hunt assistants as being derived directly from Inuit cultural and ecological skills. This last point may seem patently obvious as the nature of the travel technology and the specifics of the environment require kinds of knowledge available only to Inuit, but it is sometimes overlooked. Moreover, the sport-hunt is one of the few endeavours in which the application of traditional skills and knowledge can produce more than token remuneration for the time, energy, and money that a hunter must invest in 'land activities.'

A third observation is that, while the mail survey seemed to indicate that a part of the value visitor-hunters placed on their hunts was the quality of the overall experience with Inuit, the direct interview data seems to contradict the mail survey responses. All those interviewed felt that as much as they enjoyed the experience, including bad weather and the near constant feeling of freezing, it is securing a trophy that is paramount. As was noted earlier, only one interviewee stated that she would return to Nunavut solely for the experience of spending time with Inuit.

The first point, however, is less apparent. Outfitted hunting is, in fact, one of the few economic activities that occurs in smaller Nunavut communities that brings in significant monies (both in terms of a hunt and the overall activity) from non-government transfer payment sources, including most forms of wage employment that in most Nunavut communities are provided by government.

How significant then is such new money? If the highest and lowest fees charged in the study communities (CDN$19,000 and $14,000 respectively) are averaged, then $16,500 may be regarded as the 'standard' price of a hunt. Projecting this per hunt price to all the outfitted hunts staged in Nunavut during 2001, polar bear sport-hunting generated $1,221,000 from outside the territory into the nine communities that allocated portions of their local quotas to sport-hunters. While this amount may seem miniscule when compared to the transfer and normative wage economies of Nunavut, in places like Clyde River it is significantly more than is derived from all other tourist activities that occur in a year.

Sometimes Hunting Can Seem Like Business

Chapter Six

COMMUNITY ISSUES

Introduction

In terms of its regulatory coverage, level of monitoring and enforcement, and user adherence, the international regime adopted for the management and conservation of polar bear through the *Agreement on the Conservation of Polar Bears* (ACPB) is generally considered to be one of the most comprehensive for any arctic species (*see* Fikkan *et al.* 1993). While the system may have experienced some erosion in the last fifteen years as a result of monitoring lapses in the Russian Arctic following the collapse of the USSR, Canada has paid particular attention to creating a regime that balances consumptive use with the larger goal of resource sustainability. In short, when a conflict arises between use and conservation, the latter takes regulatory precedence.

As true as these statements are, it is also the case that the conservation regime in Nunavut has experienced some strain with respect to both subsistence and the sport-hunt use of polar bear. This is most obvious with regard to the constraints that external regulations exert on Inuit hunting and use of polar bear, and in the disparity between the fees charged by sport-hunt wholesalers *versus* the portion of those fees that flow to communities that host the sport-hunts. Indeed, problems related to both have been experienced at Clyde River and Taloyoak.

The degree to which non-Inuit, be they the small group of southern wholesalers who supply hunt clients to Inuit or the international and national regulatory and enforcement bodies, exerted control over the scale and economics of polar bear sport hunting, at the time of the research was rather localized and quite muted. The factors pertinent to the economic issues have already been detailed, while those related to the conservation/management regime that potentially affects the relationship of Inuit to polar bear throughout Nunavut will be discussed in Chapter Eight. Here the focus will be sport-hunt-related conflicts specific to and, in most cases, internal to the hosting communities that were studied. These range from disagreements between different groups of Inuit brought together into a single community by politico-historical circumstance (*see* Marcus 1992; Royal Commission on Aboriginal People 1994) to intra-community disagreements about the evolving relationship between polar bear and Inuit (and, indeed, all humans).

Before these various conflicts are explored, it should be noted that their identification is based on researcher observations and interviews with Inuit during 2001-2002. Thus, it is possible, even probable, that none, except those that relate explicitly to the exogenous control of polar bears (whether by formal policy decisions or economic arrangement), are endemic and ongoing. Indeed, some were clearly situational and of the moment, and may have been resolved or no longer at issue. Therefore, a necessary caveat in this analysis should not be generalized beyond those communities in which and at which time they have occurred. Nonetheless, they are analytically important as they, as much as the international *Agreement on the Conservation of Polar Bears* (ACPB), affect the Inuit-bear-sport-hunt dynamic.

Taloyoak and Regulatory Conflict

Inter-cultural conflicts around the sport-hunt almost invariably involve issues relating to the way the basic management of the species is conducted. The situation of Taloyoak provides a trenchant example of this type of conflict, although Gjoa Haven and Cambridge Bay, to name two other Nunavut communities, had the same experience.

Briefly, Taloyoak, which only undertook polar bear sport hunting in the mid-1990s, had both subsistence and sport hunting in the M'Clintock Channel shut down after the 2000 season. The reason for this closure was that a statistical analysis of the number of survey-marked animals appearing as a percentage of the overall harvest from the area suggested that far fewer bears were present than had been assumed when the quota of the 1990s was established. On the basis of this analysis, the estimate for the M'Clintock Channel polar bear population was revised downward from 850-900 to an estimated maximum of no more than 250 animals.

These data, when reviewed by the United States Fish and Wildlife Service (U.S.-FWS) as part of its periodic review of the status of various species and populations included under the *Marine Mammal Protection Act* (MMPA), resulted in that agency excluding M'Clintock Channel polar bear hides, including those taken through sport-hunting, from importation into the United States. As a result, American hunters, who until the year 2000 had formed the whole of Taloyoak's sport hunting clientele, ceased to book hunts for the area.

The data on depletion and the subsequent United States Fish and Wildlife Service's action also caused concern within the wildlife section of Nunavut's Department of Sustainable Development and, ultimately, the Nunavut Wildlife Management Board (NWMB). The result was that the latter, as the organization with overall responsibility for decisions regarding wildlife and harvesting in the Territory, responded by imposing a moratorium on all polar bear hunting in M'Clintock Channel. Taloyoak, however, unlike the other affected communities, has no other area to which to shift its sport-hunt (sport-hunt rights in the Gulf of Boothia were at the time reserved for outfitters based in Kugaaruk). Thus, the combined effect of the embargo and moratorium for Taloyoak meant the loss of some CDN $95,000.00 in guide and hunt-assistant wages.

The chief point of conflict in this particular case is that the original analysis that ultimately precipitated the moratorium on hunting was not discussed with the communities before these regulatory decisions were taken. Especially irksome to the Inuit is that no effort was made to incorporate or even elicit their knowledge and observations about polar bear population trends in the M'Clintock Channel at any point in the analysis or in the decision-making process.

Clyde River also experienced economic difficulties when it also underwent a drastic reduction of its annual polar bear quota from 45 to 15 animals in 1985 (Davis 1999).[1] As a result, in 1986, the community's annual quota was reduced from 45 to 21 animals. Another problem for Clyde River was that it shared the Baffin Bay polar bear population not only with two other Nunavut communities, but also with a number of Greenland communities where, in effect, nothing resembling the Nunavut management

---

[1] However, in the Clyde River case, it was the Inuit who drew attention to a possible polar bear population decline and who made the decision to reduce the quota—based on biologists' information the Inuit requested (Lloyd 1986).

institution was in place. While Nunavut wildlife managers and the Canadian Wildlife Service saw the Baffin Bay polar bear population as stable in Canada, the fact that Greenland had not developed a management plan for its portion of the area, caused the U.S.-FWS to ban the importation of polar bear trophies from this bi-nationally shared population. Clyde River continued to host a sport-hunt, but drew fewer and fewer Americans. Rather, the hunt was maintained through the late 1990s to today by drawing clients from Europe, the Middle East and Latin America.

Socio-Economic Relations in Resolute Bay

Resolute Bay developed sport-hunting as a major component of its economy in the late 1980s, in part as a response to reductions in local wage-labour opportunities. By 2000, nearly sixty percent of the Resolute Bay's annual polar bear quota was allocated to sport hunting.

While the hunt began circa 1979 as a sporadic endeavour by several community elders, it increased gradually but steadily when the Resolute Hunters' and Trappers' Association (HTA) undertook management circa 1990. Under this management system, the HTA attempted to spread both the cash and in-kind economic benefits derived from the hunt across the community. However, in 1998, a change in the executive board of the Resolute Hunters' and Trappers' Organization led to the transfer of the sport-hunt to an outfitting firm owned by a member of Resolute Bay's largest extended family.

This move to privatize the trophy hunt was prompted by several factors. The first was that this outfitting firm had developed a contract with a southern Canadian wholesaler at a significantly higher rate of remuneration per hunt ($19,000 *vs.* $14,000) than was the case for the HTO. A second was that the firm's owner and the relatives who would guide for him owned all of the dog teams in Resolute Bay. Third, with the higher contract rate, community members who relinquished their polar bear tags received greater monetary compensation ($2,000 per tag) than could be obtained by selling subsistence hunted hides through southern fur auctions. This last, as pointed out earlier, is a markedly different way of 'allocating' tags from the community quota to the sport-hunt than is done in either Clyde River or Taloyoak, where any payment for individual sport-hunt tags is retained by the HTO and used to purchase scarce items of equipment for re-sale at cost to hunters (in Clyde River) or to purchase meat and fish for low cost sale within the community (in Taloyoak).

By the end of the second year of the new outfitter-managed operation, however, a large segment of the community expressed dissatisfaction with the system**.** On the surface, the stated cause of this dissatisfaction was that the outfitter's family members were the sole recipients of most of the income generated by sport hunting. However, it also became evident that Inuit descended from Resolute Bay's northern Québec immigrant population experienced the private system as one that precluded their participation.

The understood reason for this exclusion, at least among the North Baffin Islanders who form the other segment of the community, was that Inuit originally from Northern Quebec had recently received considerable financial compensation as settlement of the 'Arctic Exiles' controversy (*see* RCAP 1994), while monies were not forthcoming to Baffin Island immigrants, including Nanuq Outfitting's owner and main employees. Not surprisingly, this situation was contentious, with the Baffin Island majority group resolved to exclude those who had received compensation for the move to Resolute Bay.

Likewise, the minority Québec-derived Inuit were aggrieved that the sport-hunt system that succeeded HTO-outfitted hunting offered almost no employment and also mandated that polar bear tags they might acquire through the lottery system be sold to Nanuq Outfitting.

Clyde River: Hunting Inuktitut

The final management issue, actually a conflict type, relates to the propriety of polar bear sport hunting and, moreover, of interventionist management. This is an issue that has recently arisen at Clyde River, but has, in fact, underlain internal community discussions since the mid-1980s and was present in the early 1970s. It reflects a perception within a part of the community that sport hunting, and indeed efforts at conservation-management, are antithetical to a respectful relationship between people and polar bears.

Doubts among Clyde River Inuit about the efficacy of management, as it was developed in the Canadian Arctic following the international ACPB, were first noted in 1973 (Wenzel n.d.). At that time, discussion by hunters, and especially elders, about the then-recently established quota system, focused not on its limit (45 animals, when in some years the take was more than 60) even though the result was a reduced harvest and some reduction in hunters' income.

Rather, the heart of the discussion was about the implied presumption that people could unilaterally influence animal behaviour, in this case by taking fewer animals than chose to make themselves available to hunters. Secondarily, it was felt that the establishment of a quota—and indeed even a population census—would make polar bears think that hunters were bragging about their own prowess and were consequently being disrespectful to *nanuq*. Such human behaviour would cause the animals to move to areas where humans would be appropriately respectful.

Despite these expressions of dissatisfaction, over the next decade Clyde hunters adhered, with only the occasional exception, to the polar bear regulations that included the imposition of closed hunting seasons, avoiding killing females with cubs less than two years of age, and hunting at denning sites. In 1985, however, Northwest Territories biologists determined that the Clyde River area had become a polar bear 'sink,' as evidenced by a harvest that was composed of animals attracted to Clyde River because the local bear population was so reduced (Davis 1999). The quota reduction from 45 to 21 bears that resulted was seen locally as tacit proof of the concerns that were expressed in the 1970s.

The sharp reduction in Clyde River's annual quota had a serious economic impact, coming so soon after the collapse of the sealskin market. Accordingly, the community undertook extended discussions, beginning in 1985 and lasting into 1987, about the costs and benefits of a polar bear sport-hunt. At this time, ideational concerns about appropriate hunter-bear relations were again widely discussed, but in 1987 the community chose to contract for visitor-hunters, with a quota of two polar bear sport-hunts that year, and increasing that number to ten by 2001-2002.

During much of this time (1987-2002), decisions concerning the numbers of tags allocated to sport-hunters and the outfitting of their hunts rested with the Hunters' and Trappers' Organization. In 1997, however, a Clyde River Inuk already established as an ecotourist guide expanded his operations to include polar bear sport-hunt outfitting, having persuaded the HTO to allocate three tags to his new business (initially he drew clients through the same southern wholesaler as did the HTO). By 2002, the number of private outfitters in Clyde River (each which was Inuit-owned) was four.

The presence of so many outfitters in the community and the availability of so few sport tags meant intense competition for clients. This vying for clients, in turn, increasingly came to be seen in the community as potentially offensive to polar bears. Because of this possibility, the HTO membership decided that in 2003 the sport allocation would be reduced to five animals and that the Hunters' and Trappers' Organization would be the sole outfitter.

The HTO's re-acquisition of the sport-hunt is recognized as an economic challenge to the individuals who had invested energy and capital as outfitters (anonymous Clyde River Inuk, personal communication 2002). However, a relatively small number of residents opposed to the sport-hunt persuaded a majority of the HTO members to reclaim the hunt. Their reasoning was two fold: first, the hunt, because it prioritizes the notion of trophy over food, offends polar bear; second, regulations that compel hunters to not hunt certain bears shows arrogance toward the animal. Thus, although economically detrimental to the local outfitters, it was felt that a deteriorating situation in human-animal relations required a new course to be followed.

There was one type of cross-cultural conflict reported in all the study communities that relate to Inuit-*Qallunaat* (Non-Inuit) relations. This conflict occurred when sport-hunters refused to hunt a bear because it was not felt by the visitor to be trophy-worthy. While only six instances of this occurrence were reported during the research, in each case the guides from those hunts recognized the inherent difference between their own polar bear hunting and that of Southerners. It was, and is, a cause of unspoken annoyance for guides, although a Clyde River guide apparently once refused to continue a hunt when the client refused bear after bear, and it was the only circumstance when Inuit mentioned that this kind of behaviour might offend polar bears.

Sometimes Hunting Can Seem Like Business

Chapter Seven

SPORT-HUNT BENEFITS AND COSTS

Benefits

From a Southern, non-Inuit vantage point, the polar bear sport-hunt is a business no different from any other entrepreneurial endeavour. The Inuit whom it employs or who otherwise facilitate it, do so for the same reason as that which motivates any person who works for a wage: to obtain sufficient money to meet life's necessities and, hopefully, also satisfy the individual's leisure pursuits.

These (especially the first), is clearly part of why Inuit communities sanction polar bear sport hunting and why some members of these communities work on trophy hunts. However, as numerous observers have pointed out (Hovelsrud-Broda 2000; Kishigami 2000; Langdon 1984. Usher 1976; Wenzel 1989, 1991, 2000), Inuit have adopted a mixed-economy model in which money is an important, but by no means the only significant, component of the economy. For Inuit, the local production of food through hunting a wide range of marine and terrestrial mammals, birds and fish is at least as important, in part because imported non-traditional foods are so expensive, and because traditional foods, that Inuit term *niqituinnaq*, possess both greater nutritional and cultural value.

The next several sections in this chapter look at the three main areas, *viz.* monetary income, food, and culture, for which Inuit receive support through their participation in the sport-hunt. And, while each is here treated independently, all three elements affect not only individuals who work as hunt guides and helpers, but have considerable import to at least large segments of their communities.

Monetary Benefits: In terms of economics, even allowing for the substantial proportion of the fee paid by a visitor-hunter to the southern expediter, the polar bear sport-hunt appears to be a beneficial situation for participating Nunavut communities and individual Inuit. The data indicate that no local outfitter experienced a financial loss in relation to the polar bear sport-hunt, although the research also makes it clear that certain marginal expenses required that an outfitter have at least three clients during a single season to be more than marginally profitable.

Similarly, those who worked as guides and helpers received net financial benefit, earning at least as much (for guides, substantially more) than would have been the case if they were employed as minimum-wage labourers in their communities. The per-hunt salaries received by dogteam guides were ca. $4,700 in Taloyoak, $5,100 in Clyde River, and $9,000 in Resolute Bay. Hunt helpers, not surprisingly, were less well remunerated, with helper salaries averaging $4,300 (range: Taloyoak average $3,800; Resolute Bay $5,000) for the duration of a hunt.

Guides from Resolute Bay and Clyde River often led at least two hunts in a season and guides and helpers in all three locations received their full salaries whether a hunt lasted its maximum time or ended successfully on its first day. Even an unsuccessful hunt did not necessarily mean any loss of salary if it was evident that a client had refused 'small bears' in hope of a 'real trophy,' or, having made that choice, was unable to obtain a trophy because of bad weather. Several such cases were reported in the course of the research, and on each occasion guides and helpers were paid in full (although sometimes gratuities and gifts were not forthcoming).

The pay received by guides and helpers is a little less impressive, however, when calculated as an hourly wage. For the 240 hours that would be worked if an outfitted hunt lasted its full limit, a Resolute Bay guide would earn $37.50/hour and his helper counterpart $20.83/hour. In each case, these are below, even well below, the hourly wages earned in Nunavut, and southern Canada, by fully qualified electricians, mechanics or plumbers (i.e., hunt guides and helpers are also skilled technicians, albeit of another sort). However, when these hourly guiding and assistant wages are compared to the hourly wage earned by a labourer working a corresponding number of hours, without overtime, at the 2001 Nunavut minimum rate of $12.00 per hour, or $2,880 for 240 hours (30 days) of work, they are impressive.

Perhaps most important of all, in terms of economic benefits derived from the sport-hunt, is that the dollars entering participating communities are large enough (and free enough) to produce benefits beyond those enjoyed by the recipient. This is not the case with transfer payments, which are usually at least partly required to be spent for specific purposes (e.g., rent or baby formula), nor with petty wages, which are received in amounts difficult to allocate usefully between daily village needs and subsistence hunting.

Sport-hunt income, however, as was shown earlier, arrives in amounts substantial enough to meet immediate 'village' needs and allow investment in the capital and/or operational costs of harvesting. Data on the amount of sport-hunt income reinvested in harvesting equipment by guides and helpers is limited to the recall of individuals regarding their use of the previous year's sport-hunt income. However, while this information is incomplete, it does suggest that the contribution that polar bear sport-hunt dollars make to the maintenance of family and community food systems through recipients' subsistence production is significant.

At Resolute Bay, about 12% of the wages earned by guides and helpers were used to buy new equipment, while at Clyde River, such purchases amounted to a full 45% of the sport-hunt wage (no data on equipment purchases were obtained at Taloyoak). Although there appears to be a large disparity between Clyde River and Resolute Bay in terms of the reinvestment of sport-hunt income, this is partly explained by the fact that two Resolute guides had purchased reconditioned mobile trailers to use as cabins. As these were at some distance from the community, their presence was unknown at the time of the interviews. While the cost of these structures was never ascertained, it was likely as much as that of a cabin constructed of imported plywood, beams, and insulation. At Clyde River, building an all-weather 3m x 7m cabin from all new materials can easily cost $7,000-8,000; the cost of one of the Resolute Bay mobile trailers was likely at least as much.

Another benefit from the sport-hunt is that communities retain all but a very small portion of the meat from visitor-hunters' sport kills. In Resolute Bay and Clyde River, where polar bear meat is a welcome part of the diet, this can be important. At Resolute Bay, the community's twenty 'sport-hunt bears' and its small Inuit population ensure that every household will receive some polar bear meat during the year. At Clyde River, this is less likely to be the case because the number of bears allocated to the sport-hunt is small relative to the number of Inuit residents. However, it was observed that both the

Hunters' and Trappers' Organization and individual guides, depending on who took responsibility to distribute meat from sport-hunts, set aside portions for elders. As was shown in Table 13, the replacement value of this meat is not insignificant, especially in the case of poorer households.

The situation at Taloyoak is somewhat different. There, polar bear is not an important part of the local diet. However, it is an important source of dog food, which costs as much as $60.00 for a 25kg bag of dry meal, and appears to be widely used by Taloyoak's dogteam owners when it is available.

The Benefits to Subsistence: In every community that stages sport hunting, the polar bear sport-hunt provides a means for these Inuit who consider themselves full-time hunters and have no desire or sometimes lack the linguistic ability to participate in full-time wage employment, to acquire important amounts of money. The importance of this to the overall subsistence system is that hunting requires prodigious amounts of time so that Inuit efforts to engage in regular wage work and daily hunting, equivalent to working two full-time jobs, is rarely successful (Wenzel 1991).

Thus, the relatively brief time that working as a guide or an assistant on a sport-hunt removes a person from food hunting, ultimately benefits the food economy of communities. This is because sport-hunt earnings are invested in equipment used to harvest 'non-cash' resources, whether seal, caribou, arctic char, small whales, or birds. These returns occur outside the time when guides and helpers appear to be 'disengaged' from traditional subsistence activities—that is, when guiding American, Norwegian, French, or Mexican visitor-hunters. Thus, it is necessary to also examine the investment priorities of hunt workers. As the following data (Table 14) from six Clyde River polar bear guides, and occasionally as helpers, show, the return in food from each sport-hunt dollar used to purchase equipment like snowmobiles is large in both material and, ultimately, socio-cultural terms.

A composite profile of the Clyde guides sub-sample shows that three of the men worked on at least ten polar bear hunts, while the other three worked seven, five, and four hunts. Five were dogteam owners, although only one currently has a working team. Five of the six, during the time that they guided (two are still active), considered themselves full-time hunters, albeit with occasional episodes as casual laborers during the summer construction period, with average individual earnings from such employment amounting to $4,000-$5,000. The sixth worked part-time as a furnace maintainer and plumber for the Clyde River's Housing Association and earned approximately $8,000 annually. One man was also a successful carver of whalebone, soapstone, and antler sculptures with annual sales of $3,000-$6000. Finally, the spouses of two, during their husbands' guiding years, had part-time hourly-wage employment from which each earned several thousand dollars.

The aggregate earnings of the six, including cash tips, from polar bear guiding was approximately CDN$183,000 (total hunts = 41), or slightly less than an average of $4,500 per hunt. The maximum earned by any individual in one sport-hunt season was $15,500. Five of the six reported using at least 50% of their sport-hunt earnings (range 44%-80%) for the purchase of major pieces of hunting equipment: snowmobiles (14—three new and 11 second-hand), five all-terrain vehicles (three new, two second-hand) and an outboard engine (new). Taken together, these equipment purchases represent about $106,000, or slightly less than 58%, of the monies earned by the six interviewees from sport-hunt employment. No estimates were solicited regarding the purchase of parts for the maintenance of this equipment or of rifles, ammunition or fuel, although each man guessed that he used in excess of $2,000 in fuel annually.

There is also another aspect with regard to the investment of sport-hunt dollars for equipment. Two of the men reported that they had transferred snowmobiles purchased with their polar bear guiding earnings to siblings who were otherwise equipment-poor. Such transfers, along with the at least occasional sharing of equipment, is worthy of note as in both instances the siblings who received the snowmobiles also functioned mainly as hunters.

Table 14: Clyde River: Sport-Hunting and Subsistence[1]

Guides (6)	Guiding Years	Total Income (guiding & other sources, or guiding alone)	Equipment Investment	Ave. Annual Harvest (kg)[2]	Ave. Annual Harvest ($)[3]	% Income to Equipment	Income : Food ($ratio)
1	5	35,000	28,000	2,360	23,600	80	1:3.4
2	10	50,000	25,000	3,400	34,000	50	1:6.8
3	5	26,000	16,000	3,160	31,600	61	1:6.1
4	10	35,000	17,000	1,980	19,800	48	1:5.7
5	7	29,000	17,000	1,800	18,000	57	1:4.4
6	4	13,100	5,800	1,120	11,200	44	1:3.4
Ave.	6.8	29,700	18,133	2,304	23,040	56	1:5.3

[1] All data are based on interviewee estimates.
[2] Edible weight of adult animals (ringed seal: 20kg, caribou: 45kg, narwhal: 100kg); note that seals used for dog feed have been excluded from calculations in Columns 5, 6 and 8.
[3] Harvest value derived as a rounded average of the cost ($10.00/kg) of the three most popular imported meats (hamburger, chicken, and pork chops) available in Clyde River's two retail stores.

Each was also asked to estimate his annual harvest production during the years he was engaged in sport-hunt work. Information was particularly sought regarding the number of ringed seals, caribou, and narwhal caught as these are three of the four main food species by edible weight in the Clyde food system (Wenzel 1991). Regarding the fourth, arctic char, no estimate was sought as none of the men felt that an accurate quantification was possible.

Taking into account that not all of the six spent the same number of seasons guiding (two men for ten years, one for only four), the following is the aggregate estimate of the six men's annual harvest of ringed seals, caribou, and narwhal during the years they received remuneration from the sport-hunt. In total, they worked 42 'seasons-years,' resulting in an estimated ringed seal catch of 3,660 animals, of which an estimated 40% was used as dog food, leaving 2,196 used as food for Clyde River residents. Similarly, the average annual harvest of caribou per individual was approximately seven animals, while the take of narwhal among the six interviewees was two and one-half animals.

The harvest from each year (ranging from four to ten years) the six men worked as conservation hunt guides or assistants was conservatively estimated at 240 ringed seals, 42 caribou, and 13 narwhal. These hunting returns provided a significant quantity of local food, estimated to be 4,800 kg of ringed seal, 1,890 kg of caribou, and 1,300 kg of *maktaaq* (the highly esteemed narwhal skin and underlying layer of fat) annually entering the Clyde River food economy in each of the years these men were employed in the sport-hunt.

The lower production of narwhal hunting, as compared to sealing and caribou hunting, appears to have several causes. In three cases, the men themselves did not own a boat and motor, while two men further stated that they had no siblings or other close kinsmen who could reliably crew with them. In fact, two men explicitly (or emphatically) stated that they did not hunt narwhal during the time when they were guides. Finally, as narwhal hunting is a highly variable activity with respect to success, it is possible that the interviewees may have participated in whaling but were unsuccessful. In summary, only two of the six reported regularly hunting narwhal with one accounting for almost two-thirds of the narwhal captured by the group.

As shown in Table 14, guides and hunt assistants contribute fresh local food valued between $3.40 and $6.80 for each $1 of remuneration obtained from the sport-hunt. This multiplier effect is a minimal figure, as it only includes a conservative estimate of the ringed seal, caribou, and narwhal harvest, and does not capture any of the value of fish and game birds harvested, nor any of the health benefits derived from replacing imported food with far more nutritious, and customary, fresh food.

Each man was also questioned about their participation in the food sharing (*ningiqtuq*) system of the community. None could quantify the amount of food they had shared, but five mentioned actively providing large amounts of all the species they harvested to the senior kinspersons in their extended families for redistribution (*see* Wenzel 1991, 1995), with three stating that they brought the entirety of their harvest return to their fathers who then redistributed it. The sixth, the oldest of the guiding interviewees, noted that he was the senior member of his family and that it was his responsibility to ensure that there was adequate food available to his grandchildrens' households.

Cultural and Other Benefits: Finally, there is a psychic or cultural benefit that certainly is experienced by those Inuit who guide or assist sport-hunters, and through their traditional skills contribute to hunter success and, sometimes, safety. None of these forms of benefit are quantifiable, but each is quintessentially Inuktitut and essential to the well-being of clients and to successful hunting.

Perhaps the most important is that by working on the sport-hunt, guides and assistants benefit from the simple fact of 'being on the land.' For older Inuit, time spent outside the communities is part of being truly Inuk. It is a time and place to exercise traditional skills that range from the actual tracking of a bear to reading the environment for hazards, to handling dogteams. Furthermore, as many of the younger Inuit who are hunt assistants may have had little opportunity to hunt polar bear, experienced hunters become tutors for the transfer of skills about both polar bear and the environment in a milieu that formal schooling and life in the communities rarely affords.

There is also a training component attached to the polar bear sport-hunt. As was noted in Chapter Four, guides frequently choose a son or other younger relative to carry out support functions on a hunt. Nearly every guide interviewed in Resolute Bay and Clyde River noted that they saw the hunt as an opportunity to introduce a young person to new land skills. Essentially, guides saw the supply person as an apprentice and the sport-hunt as an excellent place to transfer elements of the guides' traditional knowledge of bear behaviour, weather, snow and ice conditions and practical camp skills to adolescent and less-experienced hunters.

Costs

On the other hand, there are costs associated with the sport-hunt, although these, too, are difficult to quantify. They do, however, diminish the apparent gain of both an 'hourly' guiding wage that is substantially higher than that of a day labourer in Nunavut and the freedom that ten to twenty days of guiding provide in the overall scheme of individual and, even, community economy.

Socio-Cultural and Socio-Economic Costs: These costs are primarily socio-cultural. They may not always have their exact origin in the sport-hunt, but can frequently be exacerbated by it. In the context of Nunavut's small communities, these tensions cannot be considered to be insignificant. At the least, in the case of Resolute Bay, the polar bear sport-hunt has, if anything, made perceived historical inequalities between the two founding groups that constitute the Resolute Bay community starker, and seems to have created socio-cultural conflict over who has the 'right' to participate in the sport-hunt.

The sport-hunt has also highlighted the socioeconomic problems that successful participation can create when only a few individuals or a cohort of kinsmen are perceived as being the beneficiaries of sport hunting's most direct and valued product, namely a cash income. That such success can engender a negative reaction from the wider community speaks not only to the socio-politics of outfitted hunting in some Nunavut communities, but to the dialectic between the monetary and country food components in the contemporary mixed economy that prevails throughout most of Nunavut.

Economic 'Competition': Trophy hunting can also have another kind of material effect. This is that the emphasis visitor-hunters place on the taking of large male bears can have an impact on the polar bear hunting activities of Inuit not involved with sport hunting, but to whom a bear is both a source of food and a monetary resource. These Inuit access money through the sale of polar bear skins to one of several fur auctions or, occasionally, to a private buyer.

As has been discussed, the money individuals derive from such sales is far less than can be earned guiding or assisting on a sport-hunt. However, the fact that Inuit allocate far fewer animals to the trophy hunt than they could is a clear statement that polar bear hunting has importance for more than the maximum amount of money that a tag can generate. Still, the value received for a polar bear hide at auction is not insignificant to hunters.

Thus, reports by some Taloyoak and Resolute Bay Inuit of a scarcity of large male bears because of concerted sport hunting in certain areas must also be considered to be a cost. The difference in selling price of a 2.5m versus a 3m bear at fur auction can be several hundred dollars, a significant sum to hunters with limited access to other sources of money. While large female bears may still be present in areas where male animals have been reduced, the flexible quota system, with its bias against the taking of sows, may impose another limitation. Taken together, these two factors may affect optimal subsistence use in areas where 'trophy' and local hunters both seek out polar bears.

Last, outfitted hunting may bring to the surface culture-based tensions about the propriety of assisting in visitor trophy hunting. In no small way, this level of conflict is an issue between Inuit beliefs and understandings contained in *Inuit Qaujimajatuqangit* and the economic utility of polar bear trophy hunting as a producer of scarce monetary resources.

While these non-material or non-quantifiable costs can appear minor compared to the measurable benefits of sport hunting to local economies, the data presented suggest that they are by no means trivial. In each of the study communities, one or another of these non-material factors at least has worked to reduce the stability of outfitted polar bear hunting as a consistent contributor to community subsistence.

Opportunity Costs: Dowsley (2005b:3) identified another, less apparent, cost to Inuit with regard to the polar bear sport-hunt. In analyzing how polar bear tags are distributed (Table 15) at Resolute Bay, Clyde River, and Qikiqtarjuaq (formerly, Broughton Island)—each of which uses a lottery system to choose hunters—she calculated the probabilities of an individual being chosen if these communities either had no sport-hunt or did have a sport-hunt. As the table shows, the likelihood of 'winning' the lottery if some tags are allocated to sport-hunting is considerably reduced.

Table 15: Frequency of obtaining a polar bear tag in the presence or absence of the sport-hunt[1]

Community	If No Sport-Hunt		With Sport-Hunt	
	Tags/Hunters	*Frequency (yrs)*	*Tags/Hunters*	*Frequency (yrs)*
Resolute Bay	35/90	1/3	15/90	1/6
Clyde River	21/390	1/19	11/390	1/36
Qikitarjuaq	21/340	1/16	11/340	1/31

[1] *Based 2001-2002 HTO Memberships, community quotas and sport-hunt levels.*

As Dowsley shows, in Clyde River and Qikiqtarjuak, the allocation of eleven of the 21 polar bears tags for each community exacerbates an already poor subsistence situation because of the large memberships in both HTOs. Inuit in both these communities, however, have developed strategies, albeit different ones, for at least partially mitigating their respective situations.

At Clyde River, the Hunters' and Trappers' Organization membership includes a significant number of women. The enrolment of women obviously increases the probability of a household obtaining a tag (indeed, some households have two and three adult woman HTO members). In Qikiqtarjuaq, a different approach has been taken. There, the mitigation has been to expand opportunities to participate in the sport-hunt, rather than to expand the subsistence opportunity. Thus, several (usually two) polar bear tags have been designated for use in autumn sport-hunts. This has allowed members who are neither dogteam owners nor have access to a team to directly benefit from the sport-hunt allocation.

Sometimes Hunting Can Seem Like Business

Chapter Eight

MOUs, IQ AND CLIMATE CHANGE

Introduction

In the time since the polar bear sport-hunt project concluded in 2003, a number of events, some very specific to the study communities and some more encompassing in nature, have occurred that are significant with regard to the study and the overall topic. These will be first outlined and then the larger occurrences, those that are Nunavut-wide or even trans-national, will be addressed in the sections that follow.

In the communities, the changes that have taken place range from a realigning of virtually the whole of the sport-hunt operation at Clyde River to a reopening of a limited quota for Taloyoak Inuit in M'Clintock Channel. In Clyde River, the local outfitting situation has changed from the 2004 situation where four private operators were vying for the ten available sport-hunt tags, to a situation in 2005 where the Namautaq Hunters' and Trappers' Organization provided outfitting services for six clients and one remaining private operation staged four sport-hunts. Along the way, two of the three companies, A&M Tigulliraq and Qullikkut Guides Limited, ceased operation and two other local Inuit tried (unsuccessfully) to fill the gap.

The polar bear sport-hunt situation changed less in Resolute Bay and Taloyoak. However, the changes that have happened are worth notice. At Taloyoak, the loss of its quota for M,Clintock Channel was compensated for in 2005 with the community receiving an additional ten bears from the Gulf of Boothia population; presumably, the community can assign a number of its Gulf of Boothia quota to sport hunting. The Resolute Bay situation also underwent change. There, in 2003, the sport-hunt allocation was increased to twenty-five bears, with all the hunts being outfitted by Nanuq Outfitting.

While the changes noted for Clyde River, Taloyoak, and Resolute Bay have been important in their own ways for those communities, events of greater significance related to polar bear, and to sport hunting, have also occurred. The first was the completion of community negotiations in early 2005 by the Government of Nunavut and a series of Memoranda of Understanding (MOUs), one result of which was a 23% increase in the annual polar bear quota. The other was the adverse reaction to the announcement of this quota increase, initially among the scientific community and then more generally.

Nunavut's Memoranda of Understanding

The MOU approach to polar bear management in Nunavut came about through the recognition by the Territorial Government that *Inuit Qaujimajatuqangit* (Inuit knowledge and beliefs) might provide valuable information from the people most closely associated with the animal. Additionally, decisions by the Government of Nunavut regarding *IQ* made its inclusion politically expedient (*see* Government of Nunavut 1999a, b; also Wenzel 2004).

There was one additional reason influencing the MOU process. The Nunavut Government was experiencing growing pressure from Inuit communities across much of the territory for an increase in local and regional quotas. While a number of communities sought higher quotas as a way of redressing what they felt were errors in calculating the overall number of bears near these communities (Davis 1999), the predominant reason was Inuit opinion that polar bears were becoming a public safety issue, appearing in larger numbers near to or in communities and camps, especially during the ice-free period. While reliable data on polar bear-human contacts other than in hunting, are limited, interviews with Inuit make it clear that Inuit feel encounters with bears are increasing (Dowsley 2005b; Tyrrell 2007).

Indeed MOUs, as contracts between the Nunavut Government and communities about the harvesting of various species, were the product of an evolving approach to wildlife management. The earliest systematic managing of polar bear and Inuit harvesting in the NWT, initiated in the late 1960s, used Hudson's Bay Company trading ('historical') information to set annual quotas for each Inuit community. It was simplistic, but met Canada's obligations as a signatory of the *Agreement on the Conservation of Polar Bears*.

This initial approach to setting annual quotas was supplanted in the early 1990s by a 'flexible quota' system, based on improved scientific information. Whereas the historical method treated each community's polar bear harvesting as if geographically isolated from those of adjacent communities and jurisdictions, the flexible quota approach focused on managing polar bear, and hunting activities, on a more regional scale. This new approach reflected an understanding that polar bears live in relatively discrete regional populations, or demes, and an appreciation that the hunting activities of any particular community had impacts beyond that community's local area.

While the shift to a population-area schema better reflected the realities of polar bear ecology, it, like the preceding historical method, did not consider Inuit knowledge of *nanuq* in decision-making. The political environment changed with the separation of Nunavut from the Northwest Territories in 1999, creating a political jurisdiction in which Inuit comprised 85% of the residents. This new political reality mandated that Inuit Traditional Ecological Knowledge (TEK), if not all the elements of *IQ*, become a part of the wildlife management and regulatory frameworks.

The MOU process sought to remedy this absence of IQ in the earlier management approach as evidenced by several references to the role of *IQ* in the Memorandum framework (*see* Government of Nunavut 2004). The first appears under Objectives (Section 2.0/Clause 2.2) and reads, "To encourage the collection of *Inuit Qaujimajatuqangit* and scientific information on a timely basis to guide management decisions." Then in Section 7.0 (Research and Management)/Clause 7.12 which states: "*Inuit Qaujimajatuqangit* (IQ) will be incorporated in polar bear management," and that *IQ* is to assume greater management importance than had been the case is noted in 7.12(c): "The goal is that one day all the information about polar bears will be held in common as science, TEK, and IQ."

Inuit and Biologists

The completion of the Nunavut MOU process saw the annual territorial quota increased by 115 bears (28.5%), from 403 to 518 animals (*Nunatsiaq News* 2005a; Wiig 2005:1814). Within weeks, there were objections to this increase from biologists who serve on Canada's Polar Bear Technical Committee and the International Union for the Conservation of Nature' Polar Bear Specialist Group (PBSG 2005a,b).

The first problem from the biologists' perspective related to data concerning two specific populations of polar bears, those in Western Hudson Bay (WH) and in Baffin Bay (BB). In the case of the former, the Specialist Group felt that longitudinal information derived from research spanning two full decades suggested that the bear population in that area was in decline as a result of climate-related environmental changes (Stirling *et al.* 1999). Thus polar bear biologists felt that even a 5.2% quota increase (from 47 to 56 bears) as set by the new MOU would jeopardize the sustainability of WH polar bears.

Concern over the Baffin Bay polar bear population, where the quota was raised from 64 to 105 (nearly 65%), was founded on different grounds. Rather than being prompted by concerns about climate change, the Specialist Group's warning was based on new information about polar bear harvesting by Inuit hunters from Greenland's Qanaaq, Upernavik, and Scoresbysund Districts. These data suggested that the take by Greenland Inuit was substantially higher than had been estimated (Born 2005) over the preceding decade, and therefore an increase in the annual harvest by Nunavut hunters, together with further unregulated hunting by Greenlanders, would likely have a deleterious impact on that shared population.

Both groups of specialists also pointed out that in these particular cases—Baffin Bay and Western Hudson Bay—traditional Inuit knowledge was in error. This criticism seemed to also carry the wider implication: that *Inuit Qaujimajatuqangit*, while containing useful information on local situations, lacked sufficient substance for understanding regional or larger-scale polar bear population behaviour. This set of responses to the Nunavut quota increase, in turn, drew a strong reaction from Nunavut, notably an unequivocal statement by the Minister of Environment that the new allowable harvest level established through the MOUs and *IQ* as a part of wildlife policy-making were here to stay (*Nunatsiaq News* 2005b). The situation was further confused by the fact that Clause 7.12(c), while calling for TEK, *IQ* and science information on polar bears '…to be held in common…,' in its preceding sentences it states,

> Recognizing that information about polar bear population demography… and population boundaries… is not a part of IQ… scientific information on population dynamics and population boundaries will be transferred by improved communications… (Government of Nunavut 2004).

The categorical nature of statements on both sides of the MOU-*IQ*-quota issue would undoubtedly have been difficult to reconcile as each was at least tacitly questioning the basis of the other's knowledge. However, this almost immediately escalated from a disagreement between two polar bear 'specialists' groups—the Inuit and the bear biologists—to an outright clash between cultures in which Inuit ways of knowing about polar bears and their motivation for seeking a higher polar bear quota were framed by doubts about the biological sustainability of polar bear because of global climate change.

Climate Change: *IQ* and Sport Hunting vs Polar Bear

One of the more striking things about the polar-bear trophy hunt is how absent it was from the attention of North American and European conservation and animal protection organizations before January-February 2005, even among those who had opposed Inuit sealing during the 1970s and 1980s (*see* Malouf 1986). This absence in part, might be explained by the fact that the importation of polar bear to the U.S. from a number of Nunavut polar bear populations was already *MMPA*-prohibited. However, the polar-bear sport-hunt would seem a likely target given it involved killing a charismatic animal, that the hunters were wealthy 'Americans,' and that its sole purpose was to obtain a trophy—all with the pristine yet 'shrinking,' Arctic icescapes as a backdrop.

As an iconic animal, any differences between the two hunts are more of degree than kind. Nor does the difference between Canadian sealers and trophy hunters seem all that different, except for the price of the experience, which is different in kind as well as degree. In point of fact, however, it seemed that polar bear only, or principally, were of interest to Inuit, a small group of biologists, and some sport-hunters.

Invisibility ended in February 2005, as various media (*see Montreal Gazette* 2005), reported that the Humane Society of the United States (HSUS) was opposing Nunavut's newly negotiated polar bear quotas and was petitioning the U.S. Fish and Wildlife Service to considering banning trophy polar bears from Canada (apparently including any from the Northwest Territories). The reason given in the report was that Nunavut's quota increase was 'based on anecdotal evidence,' presumably observations by Inuit of their increasing encounters with polar bears.

In fact, HSUS (2005), in its press release, presented more detail about its objection, noting that polar bears are subject to pressure from climate change and the long-distance transport of pollutants into the Arctic. However, the lead sentence in the release stated that the criticism was because of plans by the Greenlandic and Nunavut governments 'for expanded trophy hunting,' a further point developed in HSUS's on-line *Marine Mammal News* stating that "…Greenland and the territory of Nunavut…announced plans to allow larger numbers of polar bears to be killed by sport-hunters" (Rose 2005). In a direct reference to Nunavut, the report also states that,

> The high demand for polar bear hunting permits is one reason why scientists are skeptical of hunters' reports of polar bear abundance—polar bear population reports have been known to be unjustifiably inflated when the demand for trophies is high (Rose 2005).

While accurate to a point—Greenland did announce shortly after the Nunavut quota increase that it was considering polar bear sport hunting (*Nunatsiaq News* 2005c, d), although it has not yet done so (but *see* HSUS 2005)—both reports erroneously attribute Nunavut's quota increase to Inuit opportunism with regard to sport hunting. As the data on outfitted hunting show, while Nunavut hunters have always been in a position to make what might be considered 'wise(r) economic use' of the polar bear's trophy potential, they have consistently not done so even in their worst economic times.

In the same way, HSUS's concern that habitat loss from climatic warming is only accurate to a point. Both of the organization's reports suggest that polar bear are universally threatened by decreased sea-ice cover. This is far beyond the IUCN Polar Bear Specialist Group (2005a) citing of Western Hudson Bay, the Beaufort and Chukchi

Seas area and East Greenland as evidencing 'unusually extensive areas of open water.' More recently, researchers (Stirling and Parkinson 2006) have suggested that the Western Hudson Bay situation may reflect conditions developing in Baffin Bay and that those polar bear may undergo the kinds of stress found among bears further south.

As for the particular threat to polar bear from sport hunting, HSUS declared that when sport hunting in Russia, Norway, Alaska and Greenland was banned under the ACPB, polar bear recovered in numbers. The last is true, but perhaps at least as significant as the sport-hunt ban in those countries was that Norway and Russia banned all hunting, including for subsistence.

Outcomes

It would be premature to present conclusions when the situation pertaining to polar bear sport hunting is so obviously still fluid. However, it is clear that post-January 2005 events have produced some recognizable short-term outcomes.

One is that the Government of Nunavut is clearly on the defensive with regard to its polar bear policy (see *Nunatsiaq News* 2005d-j). The only thing that is clear is that important attempts to meld *IQ* and non-Inuit scientific knowledge are stalled and present circumstances suggest that no single party, whether the Government of Nunavut or the IUCN Polar Bear Specialist Group can, alone, fairly impose a solution. Unfortunately, the trajectory of matters resembles the path followed in the seal controversy of the 1970s and 1980s than that of the North Alaskan Iñupiaq bowhead whale situation of the early 1980s. In the case of sealing, the scientific community was generally silent; however, in North Alaska, Iñupiaq and biologists worked together closely.

Polar bear trophy hunting, despite its economic importance to Inuit and the fact that Nunavut communities have chosen to limit sport hunting to a very modest level, will likely be jeopardized by decisions of agencies like the IUCN and U.S. Fish and Wildlife Service. The notion promoted by the Humane Society of the United States that the quotas negotiated in Nunavut were increased to expand polar bear sport hunting belies knowledge of the activity's history, most notably the degree to which trophy hunting expanded following the collapse of the sealskin trade.[1]

Even more important in the longer term is how the polar bear situation moved away from the culturally-inclusive sentiment in Clause 7.12(c) in the MOUs and became, in contrast, a general attack on *Inuit Qaujimajatuqangit*. While HSUS and media reference (*National Post* 2005) to Inuit Traditional Knowledge as consisting of anecdotes has further enlarged the cultural divide between *IQ* and science, the reality is also that neither Inuit nor members of the Polar Bear Specialist Group have publicly acknowledged the benefits that each has derived from TEK or systematic ecological research.

One tangible, and probably lasting, outcome is that the polar bear has become the poster species for global climate change, something the movement very much lacked.

---

[1] Furthermore, the Nunavut Government's recent decision to reduce the WH quota from 56 to 38 (for the 2007-08 season)and to only 8 (for the 2008-09) shows that the worst fears of the HSUS, FWS, IUCN-PBSG are unfounded – and that polar bear management in Nunavut is in responsible hands.

After all, a polar bear is more interesting than a photograph of thinning sea ice. But, in becoming a symbol for climate change, it seems to have been necessary to make it appear that polar bear (and the Arctic) are barely a heartbeat away from extinction.

Conclusions

At first glance, polar bear hunting, and especially polar bear sport hunting, might appear to have little to offer by way of insight about resource co-management. After all, polar bear hunting, to a considerable extent, is conducted under the aegis of an international convention that is welcomed by all of its signatories, and, as far as Nunavut and Canadian Inuit generally are concerned, within a regulatory framework that has both flexibility and unquestioned acceptance. In a very real sense, no northern species, possibly with the exception of bowhead whales, is as intensively managed as polar bear in terms of its use and conservation in Nunavut, or for that matter in the circumpolar world. Yet there are several important lessons to be learned from the way the sport-hunt aspect of the Inuit-polar bear relationship has evolved.

The first is that the kind of maximizing behaviour that Inuit might be expected to practice, given their recent economic history (and the present economic state of many Nunavut communities), is by no means evident. Despite being highly constrained in their ability to generate and control the monetized component of Nunavut's modern economy, Inuit have shown themselves to be optimizers with respect to the one activity able to significantly affect this situation.

While further research may reveal more subtle reasons why Nunavummiut allocate less than one-quarter of the Territory's annual polar bear quota to trophy clients, and by doing so, forego considerable scarce cash, the most apparent is cultural preference. While perhaps patently obvious, if rather simplistic, cultural reasons are supported by studies conducted in communities in East Greenland (*see* Sandell and Sandell 1996; also Robbe 1994) as well as Canada (Wenzel 1983).

The Sandells' analysis makes it clear that the Inuit in the Scoresbysund region (Kangersuttuammiut) of East Greenland view polar bear hunting as an activity conferring considerable status to individuals. During the 1970s, this was certainly also the case at Clyde River. At that time, there were two younger men (both in their mid- to late-twenties) who were known for month-long polar bear hunting trips, who would hunt bears for others and were sometimes referred to by the then settlement manager as "professional polar bear hunters" (Wenzel n.d.; Unpublished 1978 Clyde Field Notes).

The Sandells (1996:91) make another point about polar bear hunting in the Scoresbysound area that may be more trenchant. This is that for younger Inuit, polar bear hunting expresses values that are identifiably and exclusively *Inuktitut* (that is, essential Inuit cultural beliefs and values) and, as such, blunts increasingly pervasive non-Inuit influences around daily life. Not very differently, in the three Nunavut sport-hunt communities that were studied, polar bear guides took obvious pride in demonstrating their traditional land skills, from handling their dogteams to tracking bears from days-old evidence. They also frequently note that they chose a son or nephew as a helper so as to expose them to these skills and to an environment—the winter sea-ice with its myriad characteristics—in the context of pursuing an animal that is as charismatic to Inuit as it is to non-Inuit.

The latter element is very like the Sandells' (1996) description of younger men attaching themselves to knowledgeable hunters to learn polar bear hunting from them, "A prerequisite for young hunters … is that they are introduced to an area by an experienced hunter…". In Nunavut, however, this 'apprenticing' can also mean being paid. In fact, one of the Resolute Bay guides began his career with Nanuq Outfitting, working as the snowmobile assistant on hunts that were being guided by his sister.

At present, due in no small part to the way the polar bear sport-hunt industry was introduced thirty years ago, Inuit receive far less than the full commodity value (as extremely valued) of a polar bear. At present, barely one-half (<$1.5 million) of the monies actually paid by visitor-hunters to Nunavut arrives in Clyde River or Taloyoak. Still, as indicated earlier, this $1.5 Million received, for the most part, goes directly into the hands of Inuit and, in many cases to Inuit who lack 'regular' means of accessing such significant amounts of money.

Most important is that the income received by Inuit working as guides and hunt assistants has a subsistence value several times larger than the actual amount individuals receive. This is because, in many cases, it is invested in equipment essential for pursuing the whole suite of animals that comprise the Inuit food economy. To date, the exact multiplier effect of trophy-hunt dollars is not known. However, in 1999 a middle-aged Clyde River guide, used a part of his sport-hunt wages ($5,000) as a down payment for a new snowmobile, with which he caught some thirty ringed seals, six caribou, and also a significant number of arctic char (Wenzel n.d., Unpublished 2000 Clyde River Field Notes). An estimate of the quantity of nourishing and preferred food produced included approximately 750kg of seal, 300kg of caribou and, ca. 50-100kg of fish. Using the same imported food equivalency calculation as earlier, this harvest had a 'store value' of approximately $11,000.

It is germane to note that Inuit, although free to assign 100% of their polar bear quota should they wish, allocate barely 20% of the quota in any year to sport hunting. This obvious non-maximizing approach to the one 'commodity' able to generate significant monetary income from the application of traditional Inuit skills (*see* Wenzel and Bourgouin 2002 suggests that the cultural value Inuit place on polar bear hunting is decidedly more important than the purely economic return polar bears might provide.

The second point that should be emphasized is that as well-managed as polar bear are in Nunavut, conflicts arise with disconcerting frequency. The most visible and sometimes strident of these disagreements are between Inuit and management agencies.

That disagreements occur between Inuit and non-Inuit over polar bear should not be surprising. As liberally applied, if not necessarily constructed, as the management system is, it is still one in which Inuit had no original input. Further, at least in some places (*see* Davis 1999), feelings prevail that Inuit interests and concerns are still considered less than paramount. Indeed, because the *Agreement on the Conservation of Polar Bears* (ACPB) is an international accord, decisions of the other signatories affect the relationship between Inuit and polar bear across Nunavut, especially the United States through the *Marine Mammal Protection Act* (MMPA) and Greenland's lack of a management strategy for polar bear. Furthermore, that the traditional knowledge of those with by far the longest experience with polar bears seems to be only rarely incorporated into regulatory decisions or well-considered by the science that underpins it, certainly exacerbates the conflict.

There are also frictions among Inuit about the exploitation and use of polar bear. These range from issues of economic access at the local community level of Inuit involvement in the hunt, to deeply-felt cultural matters concerning the propriety of such an activity.

Socio-cultural and economic conflicts of the sort found at Resolute Bay, while somewhat unique because of that community's particular settlement history (Marcus 1992; Tester and Kulchyski 1994), are by no means absent from other communities where sport hunting takes place. And as obvious as the roots of this type of dispute may seem—namely the unequal distribution of a scarce resource—resolution of the problem has proven to be far from easy.

This is because the social group, and even more accurately the *ilagiit* or extended family, is, in fact, the traditional unit of economic production and consumption among Eastern Arctic Inuit (*see* Damas 1972a,b; Wenzel 1981, 1995, 2000). Thus, even without its particular history, the inter-group conflict seen at Resolute Bay is often played out in other communities as conflict between families, or as arose at Clyde River, between a family and community.

Probably the least tractable of the conflicts discussed here is that found in Clyde River regarding the proper use of polar bears. It is also the one that is most difficult to explain, given that its roots are exactly in the kind of ideational-symbolic relations existing between Inuit and the animal that were referred to at the start of this paper (*see also* Nuttall 1998).

In point of fact, there is no intent here toward ideational analysis or explanation, although what can be suggested is that the cultural dilemma described from Clyde River is not one that is of the either-or variety, nor one that will likely disappear. Rather, it may be an aspect of an ongoing dialogue that rises and diminishes in response to cultural, social, and economic dynamics in various communities at various times, and even in the dynamic between Nunavummiut and non-Inuit.

It is clear that polar bear sport hunting and the conflicts that arise from it are multi-layered and by no means limited to a 'simple' Inuit-outsider dichotomization of the resource and its use. Indeed, with regard to polar bear use, this is as much an issue between Inuit and contested in a uniquely cultural realm. However, this is not to say that something similar to the continuing anti-sealing campaigns that began in the 1970s and 1980s could not arise, although a 'Save the Polar Bear' campaign would likely meet with less success.[1]

Interestingly, if the matter of best, if not wise, use were strictly the province of non-Inuit decision-makers and economic planners, Nunavut Inuit might be encouraged to take fuller economic advantage of their quotas. As such, 'better' economic use would mean allocating more, if not all, of the annual quota to the sport-hunt as, at the current price per hunt paid to wholesalers (approximately CND$35,000), such a practice would inject as much as $14 Million into Nunavut's cash-poor communities. However, to receive this full amount would require that the large commission currently paid to southern wholesalers would have to be substantially reduced.

It is, therefore, a small irony that it is Inuit culture that provides something of a brake on what, in the parlance of neo-classical economics, would be a more efficient,

---

[1] The ongoing anti-sealing campaigns are sustained by the shock value of tens of thousands of 'helpless baby' seals being clubbed to death by people obviously quite different from the urban people supporting these campaigns. The polar bears' deteriorating situation is widely ascribed to global warming believed to be caused by everyone's profligate over-use of fossil fuels and not targeting only helpless baby animals.

even 'wiser' use of polar bear. In those terms, Inuit have chosen a less rational course, submerging the opportunity to maximize the monetary potential of the resource from trophy-hunter dollars in order to maintain a continuing essential cultural relationship with polar bear.

Finally, given the unique nature of polar bear hunting and the rarity of polar bear in even well-appointed trophy rooms, the loss of American hunters from certain population areas because of MMPA restriction, as in M'Clintock Channel, while certain to have short-term impact, will not end polar bear sport hunting. The situation of Clyde River since the mid-1990s attests to the fact that a polar bear trophy also draws European, Asian, and Latin American hunters to Nunavut. Undoubtedly, the overall client pool would shrink without U.S. sport-hunters, but it is also the case that hunters from other countries also have the wealth and desire to replace American clients in limited instances as has already occurred in the case of the M'Clintock Channel and Baffin Bay sport-hunts.

REFERENCES CITED

Anonymous (1972). Unpublished Clyde River Hudson's Bay Company report. Photocopy in possession of the author.

Arnakak, J. (2000). Commentary: What is Inuit Qaujimajatuqangit? *Nunatsiaq News* 25 August.

Atatahak, G. and V. Banci (2001). 'Traditional Knowledge Polar Bear Report.' Kugluktuk, Nunavut: Unpublished Report, Department of Sustainable Development, 15pp.

Boas, F. (1888). 'The Central Eskimo,' pp. 339-669 in *Sixth Annual Report of the Bureau of American Ethnology for the Years 1884-1885*. Washington, D.C.: The Smithsonian Institution.

Born, E. (2005). 'The Catch of Polar Bears in Greenland, 1993-2004.' Report to the Canadian Polar Bear Technical Committee Meeting, Edmonton, 7-9 February.

Bourgouin, F. (1998). 'The Economic Significance of Outfitted Polar Bear Hunts in Nunavut: A Preliminary Review of Information Needs for Economic Planning.' Iqaluit, Nunavut: Unpublished Report to the Department of Sustainable Development, Government of Nunavut.

Burch, E.S., Jr. (1975). *Eskimo Kinsmen: Changing Family Relationships in Northwest Alaska*. Minneapolis: American Ethnological Society Monograph No.59, West Publishing.

Collings, P., G.W. Wenzel, and R. Condon (1998). Modern food sharing networks and community integration in the Central Canadian Arctic. *Arctic* 51(4): 301-314.

DSD—Department of Sustainable Development (n.d.). 'Polar Bear Sport Hunt Summary, 1970-2000' (K-Sports.xls). Iqaluit, Nunavut: Unpublished database, Government of Nunavut, Department of Sustainable Development.

DSD—Department of Sustainable Development (2001). 'Harvest and Credit Summary, 00-01' (Harvest and Credit Summary, 00-01.xls). Iqaluit, Nunavut: Unpublished database, Government of Nunavut, Department of Sustainable Development.

Damas, D. (1963). *Igluligmiut Kinship and Local Groupings: A Structural Approach*. Ottawa: Bulletin No.196, National Museum of Canada.

Damas, D. (1969). Environment, History and Central Eskimo Society, pp. 40-64 in *Contributions to Anthropology: Ecological Essays*. Ottawa: Bulletin 230, National Museums of Canada.

Damas, D. (1972a). Central Eskimo systems of food sharing. *Ethnology* 11(3): 220-240.

Damas, D. (1972b). The structure of Central Eskimo association,' pp.40-55, in L. Guemple (ed.), *Alliance in Eskimo Society*. Seattle: American Ethnology Society.

Damas, D. (1975). Three kinship systems from the Central Arctic. *Arctic Anthropology* 12(1): 10-30.

Davis, C. (1999). 'A Case Study of Polar Bear Co-Management in the Eastern Canadian Arctic.' Saskatoon, Saskatchewan: Unpublished M.A. Thesis, Department of Geography, University of Saskatchewan.

Dick, L. (2001). *Muskox Land: Ellesmere Island in the Age of Contact*. Calgary: University of Calgary Press.

Donaldson, J. (1988). 'The Economic Ecology of Hunting: A Case Study of the Canadian Inuit.' Harvard: Unpublished Ph.D. Dissertation, Department of Organismic and Evolutionary Biology, Harvard University.

Dowsley, M. (2005a). *Inuit Knowledge Regarding Climate Change and the Baffin Bay Polar Bear Population.* Igloolik, Nunavut: Final Wildlife Report 1, Department of Environment, Government of Nunavut, 43p.

Dowsley, M. (2005b). Polar bears as a multiple use resource in Nunavut: local governance and common property conflicts. *Northern Research Forum.* http://www.nrf.is/Publications/The%20Resilent%20North/Plenary%202/3^{rdo}%20NRF-Plenary%202-Dowsley-yr-paper.Pdf

Fikkan, A., G. Osherenko, and A. Arikainen (1993). Polar bears: The importance of simplicity, pp. 96-151 in O. Young and G. Osherenko (eds.), *Polar Politics: Creating International Environmental Regimes*. Ithaca: Cornell University Press.

Foote, D.C. (1967). 'The East Coast of Baffin Island, N.W.T.: An Area Economic Survey, 1966.' Ottawa, Ontario: Unpublished Report to the Department of Indian Affairs and Northern Development, Government of Canada.

Freeman, M.M.R., ed. (1975). *Inuit Land Use and Occupancy Project*, vol. 3. Ottawa: Indian and Northern Affairs Canada.

Freeman, M.M.R., R.J. Hudson, and L. Foote, eds. (2005). *Conservation Hunting: People and Wildlife in Canada's North*. Edmonton: Canadian Circumpolar Institute Press, Occasional Publication No.56.

Freeman, M.M.R. and G.W. Wenzel (2006). The nature and significance of polar bear conservation hunting in the Canadian Arctic. *Arctic* 59(1):21-30.

Government of Nunavut (1999a). The Clyde River Protocol. www.gov.nu.ca/clyde.pdf.

Government of Nunavut (1999b). The Bathurst Mandate. (Final Draft Text: Version 7.1) www.gov.nu.ca/ Nunavut/English/department/bathurst

Government of Nunavut (2004). Polar Bear Management Memorandum of Understanding Between Qikiqtarjuaq Nativak Hunters' and Trappers' Organization, Clyde River Manautaq Hunters' and Trappers' Organization, Pond Inlet Mittimatalik Hunters' and Trappers' Organization, Qikiqtaaluk Wildlife Board and the Department of Environment For the Management of the 'Baffin Bay' Polar Bear Population. 30 January. Draft Document. Iqaluit, Nunavut: Government of Nunavut.

Hardin, R. (1999). 'Translating the Forest: Tourism, Trophy Hunting, and the Transformation of Resource Use in Central African Republic.' New Haven. CT: Unpublished Ph.D. Dissertation, Department of Anthropology, Yale University.

Harper, K. (1984). *Narwhal Tusk Market*. (Mimeo), 2pp.

Heinrich, A. (1963). 'Eskimo-Type Kinship and Eskimo Kinship: An Evaluation and Provisional Model for Presenting Data Pertaining to Inupiaq Kinship Systems.' Seattle: Unpublished Ph.D. Dissertation, University of Washington.

Holvesrud-Broda, G. (2000). 'Sharing, Transfers, Transactions, and the Concept of Generalized Reciprocity,' pp. 193-214 in Wenzel, G.W., G. Holvesrud-Broda and N. Kishigami, *The Social Economy of Sharing: Resource Allocations and Modern Hunter-Gatherers*. Osaka: Senri Ethnological Series, No. 53, National Museum of Ethnology.

HSUS—Humane Society of the United States (2005). Polar Bear Populations Under Attack in Greenland and Canada. 5 February. http://www.hsus.org/press_and_publications/press_releases/polar_bear_populations_under_attack

IUCN—International Union of the Conservation of Nature (1985). *Polar Bears.* proceedings of the Ninth Working Meeting of the IUCN/SSC Polar Bear Specialist Group, Edmonton, Alberta, 9-11 August.

Jellis, A. (1978). *Report on the Impact of Depressed Sealskin Prices in the Northwest Territories.* Ottawa: Economic Analysis Division, Department of Indian Affairs and Northern Development, 14pp.

Jenness, D. (1922). *Life of the Copper Eskimos.* Report of the Canadian Arctic Expedition 1913-1918. Ottawa, A.C. Aclund.

Jones, J.Y. (1999). *Impossible to Fail.* Franklin, TN: Hillsboro Press.

Jorgensen, J. (1990). *Oil Age Eskimos.* Berkeley: University of California Press.

Keith, D., J. Arqviq, L. Kamookak, J. Ameralik and the Gjoa Haven Hunters' and Trappers' Organization (2005). *Inuit Qaujimaningit Nanurnut: Inuit Knowledge of Polar Bears.* Edmonton: Gjoa Haven Hunters' and Trappers' Organization and CCI Press, Solstice Series No. 4.

Kemp, W.B., Wenzel, G., Jensen, N., and Val, E. (1978). *The Communities of Resolute and Kuvinaluk: A Social and Economic Baseline Study.* Toronto, ON: Polar Gas Project, 341pp.

Kemp, W.B., G.W. Wenzel, E. Val and N. Jensen (1977). *The Communities of Resolute Bay and Kuvinaluk: A Socioeconomic Baseline Study.* Toronto: Polargas Project.

Kishigami, N. (1995). Extended family and food sharing practices among the contemporary Netsilik Inuit: a case study of Pelly Bay, NWT, Canada. *Journal of the Hokkaido University of Education* 45(2):1-9.

Kishigami, N. (2000). Contemporary Inuit Food Sharing and Hunter Support Program of Nunavik, Canada, pp. 171-192 in Wenzel, G.W., G. Holvesrud-Broda and N. Kishigami, *The Social Economy of Sharing: Resource Allocations and Modern Hunter-Gatherers.* Osaka: Senri Ethnological Series, No. 53, National Museum of Ethnology.

Langdon, S. (1984). 'Contradictions in Alaska Native Economy and Society,' pp. 77-120 in Langdon, S. (ed.), *Contemporary Subsistence Economies of Alaska.* Fairbanks: Alaska Department of Fish and Game.

LATIMES. Com. (2005). Endangered Status Sought for Polar Bears. http://www.latimes.com/news/nationworld/nation/la-na-polar17feb17,0,5705416.story?coll

Lentfer, J. (1974). Agreement on Conservation of Polar Bears. *Polar Record* 17(108):327-330.

Lloyd, K. (1986). 'Cooperative Management of Polar Bears on Northeast Baffin Island.' pp.108-116 in J. Green and J. Smith (eds.), *Native People and Renewable Resource Management.* Edmonton: Alberta Society of Professional Biologists.

Malouf, A., Chair (1986). *Seals and Sealing in Canada: Report of the Royal Commission.* 3 vols. Ottawa: Supply and Services Canada.

Marcus, A. (1992). *Out in the Cold: The Legacy of Canada's Inuit Relocation Experiment in the High Arctic.* Copenhagen: IWGIA Document 71, International Work Group for Indigenous Affairs.

Milne, S., R. Tarbotten, S.Woodley, and G.W. Wenzel (1997). *Tourists to the Baffin Region: 1992 and 1993 Profiles.* Montrèal: . McGill Tourism Research Group. Industry. Report No.11, McGill University.

Montreal Gazette (2005). Animal Rights Group Questions Bear Quotas, 5 February. p.A10.

Mulrennan, M. (1997). *A Casebook of Environmental Issues in Canada*. New York: John Wiley & Sons.
National Archives of Canada (1966). Report of Cst. A.D. Kirbyson #20814 I/C Resolute Bay Det., Division 'G' Eastern Arctic, 20 July 66. RG109. Vol.19. WLT 200(5).
National Post (2005). Science Is Their Best Hope, 22 September.
Nelson, R. (1969). *Hunters of the Northern Ice*. Chicago: University of Chicago Press.
Nunatsiaq News (2001). Gunning for Bears, 10 August.
Nunatsiaq News (2003). Gjoa Haven Hunters Want Polar Bear Study Studied, 7 March.
Nunatsiaq News (2005a). Nunavut Increases Annual Polar Bear Quota By 115, 14 January.
Nunatsiaq News (2005b). Polar Bear Quotas, IQ Methods Here To Stay, 25 February.
Nunatsiaq News (2005c). Greenland Invites Polar Bear Sports Hunters, 21 January.
Nunatsiaq News (2005d). Greenland Hunt Threatens Nunavut Polar Bear Quota, 17 June.
Nunatsiaq News (2005e). Arctic Warming Threatens Polar Bears, Scientists Warn, 15 July.
Nunatsiaq News (2005f). Polar Bear Sport Hunt Under Threat from U.S, 15 July.
Nunatsiaq News (2005g). Polar Bear Quotas: Did the GN Screw Up? 15 July, (Editorial).
Nunatsiaq News (2005h). Bear Ban Bad For Business, 29 July.
Nunatsiaq News (2005i). Nunavut IQ on Polar Bears Not Documented, 5 August.
Nunatsiaq News (2005j). Boost Price for Polar Bear Hunt, Researcher Urges, 26 August.
Nuttall, M. (1998). *Protecting the Arctic: Indigenous Peoples and Cultural Survival*. Amsterdam: Gordon and Breach.
Nunavut Statistics (1999). *1999 Labour Force Survey*. Iqaluit: Nunavut Bureau of Statistics.
Nunavut Statistics (2001). *Populations Counts from the 2001 Census*. Iqaluit: Nunavut Bureau of Statistics.
Ortega y Gasset, J. (1985). *Meditations on Hunting*. New York: Scribner.
PBSG—Polar Bear Specialist Group (2005a). Resolution No.3, 14th Working Meeting of the IUCN/SSC Polar Bear Specialist Group. Seattle, 20-24 June. www.pbsg.npolar.no
PBSG—Polar Bear Specialist Group (2005b). Press Release. http://pbsg.npolar.no/Meetings/PressReleases/14-Seattle.htm
Riewe, R. (1991). *Nunavut Atlas*. Edmonton: Circumpolar Research Series No. 2, Canadian Circumpolar Institute and Tunngavik Federation of Nunavut.
Robbe, P. (1994). *Les Inuit d'Ammassalik, Chasseurs de l'Arctique*. Paris: Mémoires du Muséum National D'Histoire Naturelle, Éditions du Museum.
Rose, N. (2005). Hitting Polar Bears When They Are Down, 16 February. http://www.hsus.org/marine_marine_mammals_news/Hitting_polar_bears_when_they_are_down
Ross, W.G. (1985). *Arctic Whalers, Icy Seas: Narratives of the Davis Strait Whale Fishery*. Toronto: Irwin.
RCAP—Royal Commission on Aboriginal People (1994). *The High Arctic Relocation: A Report of the 1953-1955 Relocation*. Ottawa: Supply and Services Canada.
RCMP—Royal Canadian Mounted Police (1969). Clyde River Detachment Report to G. Division. Photocopy in possession of the author.
Sandell, H. and B. Sandell (1996). Polar bear hunting and hunters in Ittoqqortoormiit/Scoresbysund, NE Greenland. *Arctic Anthropology* 33(2):77-93.

Smith, P.A. (1977). *Resume of the Trade in Polar Bear Hides in Canada, 1975-76*. Ottawa: Progress Note 82, Canadian Wildlife Service.

Smith, P.A. (1978). *Resume of the Trade in Polar Bear Hides in Canada, 1976-77*. Ottawa: Progress Note 89, Canadian Wildlife Service.

Smith, P.A. and C. Jonkel (1975a). *Resume of the Trade in Polar Bear Hides in Canada, 1972-73*. Ottawa: Progress Note 43, Canadian Wildlife Service.

Smith, P.A. and C. Jonkel (1975b). *Resume of the Trade in Polar Bear Hides in Canada, 1973-74*. Ottawa: Progress Note 48, Canadian Wildlife Service.

Smith, P.A. and I. Stirling (1976). *Resume of the Trade in Polar Bear Hides in Canada, 1974-75*. Ottawa: Progress Note 66, Canadian Wildlife Service.

Stevenson, M. (1997). *Inuit, Whales, and Cultural Persistence: Structure in Cumberland Sound and Central Inuit Social Organization*. Toronto, ON: Oxford University Press.

Stevenson, M. (1995). *Inuit Whalers and Cultural Persistence: Structure in Cumberland Sound and Central Inuit Social Organization*. Toronto: Oxford University Press.

Stirling, I., N. Lunn, and J. Iacozza (1999). Long-term trends in the population ecology of polar bears in Western Hudson Bay in relation to climate change. *Arctic* 52(3): 294-306.

Stirling, I. and C. Parkinson (2006. Possible effects of climate warming on selected populations of polar bears (*Ursus maritimus*) in the Canadian Arctic. *Arctic* 59(3): 261-275. rt Hunt Amendment to the U.S. *Marine Mammal Protection Act* on Polar Bea

Taylor, M. (1999). Effects of the Polar Bear Sport Conservation in Canada. Unpublished Draft Report in possession of the author.

Taylor, M. and J. Lee (1995). Distribution and abundance of Canadian polar bear populations: a management perspective. *Arctic* 48(2): 147-154.

Taylor, M., J. Laake, P. McLoughlin, E. Born, H. Cluff, S. Ferguson, A. Rosing-Asvid, R. Schweinsburg and F. Messier (2005). Demography and viability of a hunted population of polar bears. *Arctic* 58(2): 203-214.

Tester, F. and P. Kulchyski (1994). *Tammarniit (Mistakes): Inuit Relocation in the Eastern Arctic 1939-63*. Vancouver: UBC Press.

Tyrell, M. (1986). More bears, less bears: Inuit and scientific perceptions of polar bear populations on the west coast of Hudson Bay. *Études/ Inuit /Studies* 30(2): 191-208

U.S. Government (2001). *List of Polar Bear Populations Approved for the Import of Sport-Hunted Trophies by Permit from the Northwest Territories (NWT) and Nunavut, Canada*. Arlington: U.S. Fish and Wildlife Service, 1p. (mimeo).

Usher, P. (1976). Evaluating country food in the northern Native economy. *Arctic* 29(2): 105-120.

Usher, P. (2000). Traditional ecological knowledge in environmental assessment and management. *Arctic* 53(2):183-193.

Wenzel, G.W. (1981). *Clyde Inuit Ecology and Adaptation: The Organization of Subsistence*. Ottawa: Canadian Ethnology Service Paper No.77, National Museums of Canada.

Wenzel, G.W. (1983). Inuit and polar bears: an example of cultural resource use from Resolute Bay. *Arctic* 36(1): 90-95.

Wenzel, G.W. (1989). Sealing at Clyde River, N.W. T.: a discussion of economy. *Études/Inuit/Studies* 13(1): 3-23.

Wenzel, G.W. (1991). *Animal Rights, Human Rights: Ecology, Economy and Ideology in the Canadian Arctic*. Toronto: University of Toronto Press.

Wenzel, G.W. (1995). Ningiqtuq: Inuit resource sharing and generalized reciprocity in Clyde River, Nunavut. *Arctic Anthropology* 32(2): 43-60.

Wenzel, G.W. (1997). Using harvesting research in Nunavut: an example from Hall Beach. *Arctic Anthropology* 34(1): 18-28.

Wenzel, G.W. (2000). 'Sharing, Money, and Modern Inuit Subsistence: Obligation and Reciprocity at Clyde River, Nunavut,' pp. 61-85, in G.W. Wenzel, G. Hovelsrud-Broda and N. Kishigami (eds.), *The Social Economy of Sharing: Resource Allocation and Modern Hunter-Gatherers*. Osaka: Senri Ethnological Series No.53, National Museum of Ethnology.

Wenzel, G.W. (2004). From TEK to *IQ*: Inuit Qaujimajatuqangit and Inuit cultural ecology. *Arctic Anthropology* 41(2): 238-250.

Wenzel, G.W. (2005). 'Nunavut Inuit and polar bear: the cultural politics of the sport hunt,' pp.363-388 in Kishigami, N. and J. Savelle (eds.), *Indigenous Use and Management of Marine Resources*. Osaka: Senri Ethnological Series No.67, National Museum of Ethnology.

Wenzel, G.W.(n.d.). Unpublished Clyde Field Notes, 1971-1978, 1984-1987, 1991-1999, 2001.

Wenzel, G.W. and F. Bourgouin (2002). 'Polar Bear Management in the Qikiqtaaluk and Kitikmeot Regions of Nunavut: Inuit, Outfitted Hunting and Conservation.' Iqaluit, Nunavut: Unpublished Report to the Department of Sustainable Development, Government of Nunavut.

Wenzel, G.W. and M. Dowsley (2005). 'Economic and cultural aspects of polar bear sport hunting in Nunavut, Canada,' pp.37-45 in Freeman, M.M.R., R.J. Hudson, and L. Foote (eds.), *Conservation Hunting: People and Wildlife in Canada's North*. Edmonton, AB: CCI Press, Occasional Publication No. 56.

Wenzel, G.W., M. Dowsley and M. Trudeau (2005). *Polar bear Sport Hunting in Nunavut: Why It Is Not A Win-Win Situation For Inuit*. Poster Presented at the Society for Economic Anthropology 2005 Annual Meeting, Hanover, New Hampshire, 21-23 April.

Wenzel, G.W. and L.-A. White (2000). 'Chaos and Irrationality: Money and Inuit Subsistence Practice.' Unpublished Paper Presented at International Congress of Arctic Social Sciences IV, Québec City, 16-20 May.

White, L.-A. (2000). 'Clyde Inuit Subsistence, Sharing and Money.' Unpublished Manuscript (cited with permission of the author).

Williamson, R. (1977). *The Boothia Peninsula People: Social Organization in Spence Bay, Northwest Territories*. Saskatoon, Sask: University of Saskatchewan Institute for Northern Studies Polar Gas Socio-Economic Program.

Wiig, Ø. (2005). Are Polar Bears Threatened? *Science* 309 (16 September), pp. 1814-1815

APPENDICES

Following completion of the research contained in this report, two sets of recommendations were transmitted orally to the Government of Nunavut, to Nunavut Tunngavik Incorporated, and to the Clyde River, Taloyoak, and Resolute Bay Hunters' and Trappers' Organizations executive committees. The first pertained specifically to the polar bear sport-hunt as found in each of the study communities, and suggested no structural changes to the organizational aspects of this activity. Rather, that recommendation focused on how sport hunting might support the flexible quota system. As such, it was modest in scope.

The second set of recommendations grew out of reflections on the economic relations attending sport hunting as it was being conducted during the research. Its focus was on the economic development potential of polar bear sport hunting and, therefore, on structural aspects of the activity. It was more expansive in its scope than the first recommendation.

Sometimes Hunting Can Seem Like Business

Appendix One

Recommendations

Recommendation to the Government of Nunavut

Because a number of communities have incurred penalties under the flexible quota approach to polar bear management due to accidental 'overharvesting' of female bears, it might be useful to consider formally restricting the sport take of polar bear to male animals. To do so will likely impose no hardship on trophy seekers as the general ethos among sport-hunters favours the taking of male bears. Furthermore, because of the heavy reliance for the success of such a regulation on Inuit Traditional Ecological Knowledge, it may make the development of an apprentice guide system desirable so that younger men who aspire to be polar bear guides can acquire this expert knowledge through direct experience. Another benefit of such a system is that it would contribute to the transmission of TEK information about bears more generally and bear habitat and ecology to younger generations of hunters.

Additional Recommendations

Polar bear sport hunting brings considerable sums of 'new' money into those communities that choose to host client-hunters. However, as the outfitted hunting system presently functions, with clients being directed to communities via southern-based wholesalers, the wholesaler now retains 40% or more of the overall fee. It would be to the obvious advantage of those communities engaged in sport hunting programs if a larger amount of money came into the North.

One possible way of accomplishing this would be for Inuit to assume the role played by wholesalers. However, for each community to develop the contacts needed to operate independent of wholesalers is unrealistic, if only because no community or local outfitter has the financial resources to do so.

On the other hand, a centralized authority or group in Nunavut, possibly the Government of Nunavut or Nunavut Tourism, might fulfill such a role. Even more preferable would be for Nunavut Tunngavik Inc. to fill this niche. There are several reasons for centralizing this activity and for NTI or another Inuit-operated business organization to be the agency, but this will be returned to later.

Whatever the agency that fills the 'wholesaler' role, it would first have to establish contacts with sport-hunters through advertising in publications and websites serving the sport-hunt community, and by being present at events like the Safari Club International convention. This last would be costly, but also relatively short-term.

At the same time that these contacts are being established, a web-based electronic auction system should also be developed. This will be the means for the actual sale of hunts. All communities intending to host sport-hunts would post this information on the auction website.

In outline, once their HTOs have set the local sport-hunt allocation and season, the basic form of operation would be for those communities that share the same polar bear population (for example, Clyde River, Qikiqtarjuaq, and Pond Inlet in regard to the Baffin Bay polar bear population), to simultaneously post perhaps two bears each for the first hunt of the season. A starting bid level (the overall price paid when hunts are arranged through southern wholesalers) would be set and bids accepted at or above that starting price. Each tag posted would be available for bidding for forty-eight hours and the bidding would be updated every two hours. Currently, e-Bay offers an example of this. The bidding process would be repeated until all the allocated tags are sold.

Ideally, such an approach will have several advantages over the present system. The most obvious is that it has the potential to at least bring North the entire fee paid by sport-hunters, including the wholesaler's 'commission.' There is also the possibility that such a system may ultimately bring higher per bear prices.

Second, it can mean more bears become available to be hunted by Inuit, as a higher per bear price will allow communities to sell fewer tags to sport-hunters while making more money overall. As the present lottery system for distributing 'subsistence' tags can mean an individual may not be able to hunt polar bear for years, each additional tag available through the lottery increases the overall opportunities for individuals to hunt polar bears.

Third, a centralized auction system does not necessarily mean a change in any community's way of outfitting sport-hunts. Sport tags can still be allocated to a local private outfitter. The difference is that the wholesaler will be based in the North. But centralization will also ensure that neither communities nor outfitters will undercut each other by competing for clients.

Last, this approach can directly contribute to polar bear conservation. In light of higher sport earnings and a possibly larger subsistence hunt, it would be politically advantageous for those communities that stage sport-hunts to voluntarily 'give back' one bear from the community quota for conservation purposes. This is suggested for the simple reason that sport hunting is generally unpopular in Europe, the United States, and southern Canada and such a 'give back' would deny southern anti-hunting organizations any political or moral advantage whilst further justifying the conservation hunting nature of the Canadian polar bear sport-hunt.

Returning to what agency might function as the wholesaler, NTI seems to be the one organization that has the political capital required to persuade communities and local outfitters to participate in such a proposal. To offset the costs of maintaining the auction and so forth, a 'wholesaler fee' of 15% would go to the managing organization for maintenance of the system.

Appendix Two

Objectives, Data Types, and Methods

Research

The research reported here was designed (*see* Wenzel and Bourgouin 2002) to acquire data relevant to two questions. The first of these concerned whether sport hunting for polar bear can play a (larger) strategic role in the conservation and management of that species. The second was to determine the economic benefits received by Inuit and their communities from the polar bear sport-hunt. With regard to the last, the study examined Inuit participation in polar bear sport hunting in terms of both its monetary and socio-cultural importance.

In designing a program of research capable of meeting these objectives, two main assumptions were accepted. The first was that species' conservation and sustainable use would remain the principal tenet of the Government of Nunavut's cultural, economic and scientific policies regarding polar bears. The second was that for Inuit, the cultural, economic, and social aspects of polar bear hunting, including that carried on by visitors seeking tangible trophies, are equally intertwined.

The Data

In order to achieve these objectives, the research effort was directed at the development of several interrelated datasets. The most important of these concerned the fees and expenses associated with polar bear sport hunting as it is presently conducted and, of course, the income derived by Nunavummiut (residents of Nunavut). Thus, of primary importance was information on the wholesale cost of a hunt purchased through southern providers, the amount or proportion of this sum accruing to community-based outfitters in Nunavut, and the wages then received by hunt employees (guides, supply assistants, clothing and hide preparers).

In addition to the above, various types of 'secondary' economic data were also collected. These included non-package expenditures by visiting hunters (individually-purchased equipment in the local community, gratuities, and local arts and crafts purchases) and the operational costs (insurance, fuel and food) of outfitters and guides. Furthermore, the research also investigated whether and to what degree the sport-hunt affects the hiring patterns of community enterprises, and how individuals working in the industry, including within the informal economy, expend sport-hunt revenues. This last aspect was especially concerned with how sport-hunt monies earned by Inuit contributed to the overall subsistence system either through (1) the direct investment by sport-hunt workers of their earnings in equipment used in hunting generally, or (2) the normative 'sharing' of sport-hunt earnings and/or employment opportunities (Wenzel 1989, 2000; Wenzel and White 2000).

Finally, to better understand how the 'new' money that polar bear sport hunting brings to hosting communities circulates through informal mechanisms, the research also examined the socio-economic and socio-political dimensions of this activity in the three communities that were studied—Clyde River, Resolute Bay, and Taloyoak. This was undertaken in order to determine if the cultural institutions that facilitate the flow of traditional resources and products associated with Inuit harvesting serve a similar distributive function using the money produced by the sport-hunt.

A number of qualitative datasets were also developed. The first concerned the attitudes of Inuit (both those working in and those with no connection to their local sport-hunt) in the study communities toward polar bear sport hunting. Of particular concern were the perceptions of individuals regarding the benefits and negative effects of sport hunting to their communities, their experiences with visiting hunters, and the overall propriety of the trophy hunt as understood by these informants. Information was also sought from a sample of southern hunters who had contracted polar bear hunts about their experiences while in Nunavut. Here, data on visitors' satisfaction with local services, the ease or difficulty of communicating with Inuit outfitters, guides and helpers, the quality of food and equipment provided during their stay, and the preparedness of outfitters and guides were solicited.

Another element of the project focused on the traditional knowledge of polar bear behavior that Inuit involved in sport-hunt guiding brought to or employed in the course of this activity. The emphasis in this study component centred on practical or factual aspects of 'traditional ecological knowledge' (TEK) which, in the context of this study, refers to Inuit observations about the biology and ecology of polar bear used to facilitate sport-hunt events, rather than on the ideological-cultural aspects of Inuit knowledge concerning polar bears.

Appendix Three
Data Collection

Data Collection

All data were collected under Nunavummi Qaujisaqtulirijikkut (Nunavut Research Institute) Scientific Research License No.0500501N-A. The collection of primary community information was carried out at Resolute Bay and Taloyoak in April-May, 2001, and at Clyde River in September 2001, with limited follow-up in Clyde River and Resolute Bay in 2002. Secondary data, primarily from the Government of the Northwest Territories and Nunavut Government archives and databases, were gathered, respectively, in Yellowknife, Northwest Territories, in May 2001 and in Iqaluit, Nunavut, in October 2001.

Two methods were employed in fulfilling the project's data requirements. These were semi-structured interviews and self-reporting mail surveys.

Semi-structured interviews, using a protocol pre-tested during the summer of 2000, before actual data collection began, were the chief research tool used in each of the three study communities. Pre-testing was essential, allowing the research team both to determine the appropriateness of the questions ultimately included in the protocol and, more importantly, to learn how to 'pace' the interviews.

All interviews were conducted face-to-face and, depending on the interviewee's experience and preference, lasted between thirty minutes to one and one-half hours, exclusive of the informed consent procedure (see below). Ideally, each interview was completed in one session, but in a number of instances two, and in two cases three, sessions were required. Most interviews were conducted in respondents' homes and proceeded only after the research objectives and interview procedure were explained and signed informed consent obtained. Interviewees were paid $50.00 per session hour or part of an hour, although any mention of payment was withheld from those approached for interviews until the conclusion of a session in order not to unduly influence participation. Only one person declined from participating.

The interview instrument used was a questionnaire (presented in both Inuktitut and English versions), divided into several sections specific to the data categories being sought. Thus, there were sections pertinent to an interviewee's particular experience with sport hunting and sport-hunters (whether as a guide, outfitter, supply assistant, general observer, and so forth). In addition, other major sections focused on an individual's observations about bears (TEK), aspects of hunt employment, the economic benefits of sport hunting, and perceptions about the current regulatory and local circumstances under which sport hunting takes place.

The second means of primary data collection was through a questionnaire-based survey directed at non-Inuit sport-hunters who had participated in polar bear hunts in Nunavut, (or the Northwest Territories if the hunt took place prior to 1999 when Nunavut became a separate political jurisdiction). The survey was mainly administered by post in order to reach 156 men and women from eleven countries who had hunted polar bear in the Canadian Arctic between 1992 and 1999. Because of the time interval between our contact with individuals and when their hunts had occurred (as noted above, in some cases eight years), the information thus received was approached as potentially 'biased' recall, due to the elapsed time. However, as will be discussed in the Sport Hunter Profile section of this report, data pertinent to matters such as the package fee paid to southern providers and the advertised maximum duration of hunts were found to be generally consistent and, thus, presumably reliable.

Confidence in this recall reliability was further strengthened by cross-checking mail survey data against hunt information collected from eleven sport- hunters encountered in Resolute Bay and Clyde River during the April and May 2001, community research visits. Each of these interviews was conducted using the same questionnaire as was sent to the large mail survey group the preceding autumn. However, field interviews with sport-hunters solicited additional information not included in the mail survey, such as the number of days lost to weather and whether a snowmobile was used to return to the hosting community at the hunt's end. The responses from sport-hunters interviewed in Clyde River and Resolute Bay were found to be consistent with those given on the same topics in the returned mail surveys.

Finally, additional information on sport-hunters' perspective of the Nunavut experience was acquired through follow-up interviews conducted with fourteen individuals attending the XXIX Safari Club International convention in January 2001. This group was self-selected, and comprised mail survey respondents who agreed to a follow up interview at the convention.

Two additional types of data were also obtained. The first concerned information about the hunt pricing by southern providers, their modes of advertising, and the associated costs. Data were also sought on the percentage commission retained by the provider relative to the fee paid to private or community outfitting organizations in Nunavut. To this end, several hunt providers were interviewed during the Safari Club convention in 2001. Further, data specific to the contractual relationship between southern wholesalers and northern communities/organizations were obtained by examining letters of agreement and contracts between these providers and their Nunavut community contacts.

Finally, data on the benefits of the sport-hunt as these might be reflected in the seasonal hiring of hotel service personnel or through increased local art-handicraft production and sales were also gathered. The primary sources for such information were the management personnel of various community businesses (the Federated Co-operative and/or Northern stores) in the study communities, Hamlet Senior Administrative Officers, Hunters' and Trappers' Organization hunt coordinators, and local artisans.

EXTENDED TABLE OF CONTENTS

Table of Contents i
Preface iii
    About the Project iii
Acknowledgements v

Chapter One:
THE STUDY COMMUNITIES 1
Introduction 1
Fig. 1. *Nunavut study sites* 2
Fig. 2. *Canadian polar bear population zones* 3
Community Baseline Information 4
    Clyde River 4
    Fig. 3. *Clyde River* 4
    Resolute Bay 5
    Fig. 4. *Resolute Bay* 6
    Taloyoak 6
    Fig. 5. *Taloyoak* 7
Summary 8

Chapter Two:
POLAR BEARS AS A RESOURCE: AN OVERVIEW 9
Inuit Subsistence 9
The Commodization of Polar Bears: Circa 1850-1970 9
The Business of Polar Bear Sport Hunting: 1970-1985 11
    Table 1: Northwest Territories Community Polar Bear Quotas—1973 ... 12
The Contemporary Sport-Hunt: 1985-2000 14
    Table 2: Annual Quota and Sport Harvest, 1970-2000 15
    Table 3: NWT-Nunavut Polar Bear Population Area and Sport-Hunts,
        1970-2000 17
    Table 4: Success Rate for Polar Bear Sport-Hunts in Four Canadian
        Population Areas 18
    Table 5: Current MMPA Import Status of Nunavut–NWT Polar
        Bear Populations 19
Summary 19

Chapter Three:
INUIT TEK AND THE SPORT-HUNT 21
Traditional Ecological Knowledge (TEK) 21
TEK in the Present Research 21
The Management System 22
TEK and Polar Bear Conservation 23
TEK and the Sport-Hunt 24
    Table 6: Male-Female Sport Harvest Ratio in the Study Area 25

The TEK Data ... 26
    Table 7: Characteristics of Sport-Hunt Workers ... 26
    Abundance ... 26
    Table 8: Polar Bear Abundance: Sample Responses ... 27
    Identifying Gender ... 28
    Table 9: Polar Bear TEK Gender Identification: Sample Responses ... 29
Traditional Knowledge Summary ... 31

Chapter Four:
COMMUNITY ORGANIZATION OF THE HUNT ... 33
An Introductory Perspective ... 33
    Table 10: Sport Hunter Characteristics ... 33
Community Dynamics and *Inuit Qaujimajatuqangit* ... 34
    Resolute Bay ... 35
        Hunt History ... 35
        Fig. 6. *Resolute–Barrow Strait sport-hunt areas* ... 36
        The Basics of the Resolute Sport-Hunt ... 38
        Nanuk Outfitting ... 38
        Table 11: Outline of the Resolute Bay Sport-Hunt ... 39
        Visitor-Hunters ... 40
        Guides and Helpers ... 40
        Meat Sharing ... 42
        IQ and the Resolute Bay Sport-Hunt ... 42
    Clyde River ... 44
        General Features of the Sport-Hunt ... 43
        Sport-Hunt Organization at Clyde River ... 44
        Fig. 7. *Clyde River-Baffin Bay sport-hunt areas* ... 45
        Clyde River's Outfitters ... 47
            Namautaq HTO ... 47
            Qullikkut Guides Ltd., (QGL) ... 48
            Clyde River Trophy Hunts (CRTH) ... 48
            A&M Tigulliraq (A&MT) ... 49
            An Overview of Outfitting ... 49
            Clyde River Hunt Clients ... 50
            The Guides and Helpers ... 50
            IQ and Outfitting in Clyde River ... 52
    Taloyoak ... 53
        Hunt Overview ... 53
        Outfitting ... 54
        Fig 8: *Taloyoak sport-hunt areas (2000)* ... 55
        The Hunt Clients ... 56
        The Lead and Ski-Doo Guides ... 56
        IQ at Taloyoak ... 58
        Ethnographic Summary ... 58

Chapter Five:
SPORT HUNTING AND INUIT SUBSISTENCE ... 61

Introduction 61
Overview of the Data 61
Pattern of the Analysis 62
The Sport-Hunt's Values and Flows 63
    A) Demand Value 63
    B) Price 64
The Southern Data 64
    A) The Hunters 64
    B) The Wholesalers 66
The Northern Data 67
    A) Local Outfitters 67
    B) Guides and Helpers 68
    C) Other Workers 70
    D) Other Hunt Benefits 71
Section Summary and Observations 73
    Table 12: Generalized Pattern of Outfitted Hunts 73
    Table 13: Economic Attributes of Polar Bear Sport Hunting 74

Chapter Six:
COMMUNITY ISSUES 77
Introduction 77
Taloyoak and Regulatory Conflict 78
Socio-Economic Relations in Resolute Bay 79
Clyde River: Hunting Inuktitut 80

Chapter Seven:
SPORT HUNT BENEFITS AND COSTS 83
Benefits 83
    Monetary Benefits 83
    The Benefits to Subsistence 85
    Table 14: Clyde River Sport-Hunting and Subsistence 86
    Cultural and Other Benefits 87
    Table 13: Economic Attributes of Polar Bear Sport Hunting 74
Costs 88
    Socio-Cultural and Socio-Economic Costs 88
    Economic Competition 88
    Opportunity Costs 89
    Table 15: Frequency of Obtaining a Polar Bear Tag in the Presence
        Or Absence of the Sport-Hunt 89

Chapter Eight:
MOUs, IQ AND CLIMATE CHANGE 91
Introduction 91
Nunavut's Memoranda of Understanding 91
Inuit and Biologists 92
Climate Change, *IQ* and Sport Hunting vs Polar Bear 94
Outcomes 95

CONCLUSIONS **97**

REFERENCES CITED **101**

APPENDICES **107**
Appendix One: Recommendations
    Recommendation to the Government of Nunavut 109
    Additional Recommendations 109
Appendix Two:
    Research Objectives, Data Types, and Methods 111
    The Data 111
Appendix Three:
    Data Collection 113

EXTENDED TABLE OF CONTENTS **115**
    List of Tables 118
    List of Figures 118
    Glossary of Frequently Used Abbreviations 119

List of Tables

Table 1 Northwest Territories Community Polar Bear Quotas—1973 12
Table 2 Annual Quotas (AQ) and Sport Harvests (SH), 1970-2000 15
Table 3 Growth of Polar Bear Sport Hunting in NWT-Nunavut, 1970-2000 17
Table 4 Successful *vs* All Sport-Hunts in Four Population Areas 18
Table 5 MMPA Status of NWT–Nunavut Polar Bear Populations 19
Table 6 Male:Female Sport Harvest Rations in the Study Areas 25
Table 7 Characteristics of the Sport-Hunt Workers 26
Table 8 Polar Bear Abundance: Sample Responses 27
Table 9 Polar Bear Gender Identification: Sample Responses 29
Table 10 Sport Hunter Characteristics 33
Table 11 Outline of the Resolute Sport-Hunt 39
Table 12 The Pattern of Outfitted Hunts 73
Table 13 Economic Attributes of Polar Bear Sport Hunting 74
Table 14 The Sport Hunt and Clyde River Subsistence 86
Table 15 Frequency of Subsistence Tag Selection 89

List of Figures

Figure 1. Nunavut Study Sites 2
Figure 2. Canadian Polar Bear Population 3
Figure 3. Clyde River 4
Figure 4. Resolute Bay Areas 6
Figure 5. Taloyak Areas 7
Figure 6. Resolute–Barrow Strait Sport-Hunt Areas 36
Figure 7. Clyde River–Baffin Bay Sport-Hunt Areas 45
Figure 8. Taloyoak–M'Clintock Channel Sport-Hunt Areas 55

GLOSSARY OF FREQUENTLY USED ABBREVIATIONS

A&MT	A &M Tiqulliraq
ACPB	*Agreement on the Conservation of Polar Bears*
ANL	Adventures Northwest Ltd.
CITES	Convention on International Trade in Endangered Species
CNO	Canada North Outfitting
CRTH	Clyde River Trophy Hunts
DFO	Department of Fisheries and Oceans (Canada)
DIAND	Department of Indian Affairs and Northern Development
EU	European Union
GN	Government of Nunavut
GNWT	Government of the Northwest Territories
HBC	Hudson`s Bay Company
HSUS	Humane Society of the United States
HTA	Hunters and Trappers Association
HTO	Hunters and Trappers Organization
IQ	Inuit Qaujimajatuqagit
IUCN	International Union for the Conservation of Nature
MMPA	*Marine Mammal Protection Act*
MOU	Memorandum of Understanding
NLCA	*Nunavut Land Claims Agreement*
NTI	Nunavut Tunngavik Incorporated
NWMB	Nunavut Wildlife Management Board
PBTC	Polar Bear Technical Committee
PBSG	Polar Bear Specialist Group
QGL	Qullikkut Guides Ltd.
RCMP	Royal Canadian Mounted Police
SCIF	Safari Club International Foundation
TAH	Total Allowable Harvest
TEK	Traditional Ecological Knowledge
USF&WS	United States Fish and Wildlife Service